BrightRED Study Guide

Curriculum for Excellence

N5

MODERN STUDIES

Kirsty Marsland, Caleb Marwick and Heidi Stoutjesdyk

Contributing editor Derek Timpany

First published in 2013 by:
Bright Red Publishing Ltd
1 Torphichen Street
Edinburgh
EH3 8HX

A CIP record for this book is available from the British Library.

ISBN 978-1-84948-321-6

With thanks to:
PDQ Digital Media Solutions Ltd, Bungay (layout), Anglosphere Editing Ltd (editorial). Cover design and series book design by Caleb Rutherford – eidetic.

Acknowledgements
Every effort has been made to seek all copyright-holders. If any have been overlooked, then Bright Red Publishing will be delighted to make the necessary arrangements.

Permission has been sought from all relevant copyright holders and Bright Red Publishing is grateful for the use of the following:

Logos © The Conservative Party, The Labour Party, The Liberal Democrats & The Scottish National Party (p 8); Ian Murray (p 9); Caleb Marwick (p 10); Two Parliamentary copyright images reproduced with the permission of Parliament (p 12); UK government (OGL v.3)[1] (p 15); Duirinish Light/Shutterstock.com (p 18); Two images © Scottish Parliamentary Corporate Body – 2012. Licensed under the Open Scottish Parliament Licence v1.0. (pp 19 & 20); MrPenguin20/Creative Commons (CC BY-SA 4.0)[2] (p 24); Lance Bellers/Shutterstock.com (p 24); Alanatabz/Creative Commons (CC BY-SA 4.0)[2] (p 25); Ad Meskens/Creative Commons (CC BY-SA 3.0)[3] (p 25); Malcolm Bell (p 26); Mandy Morgan (p 26); M J Richardson/Creative Commons (CC BY-SA 2.0)[4] (p 27); Malcolm Bell (p 27); Cara Hilton (p 28); Estillbam/Creative Commons (CC BY-SA 3.0)[3] (p 29); MrPenguin20/Creative Commons (CC BY-SA 4.0)[2] (p 34); Logos © The Conservative Party, The Scottish National Party, The Labour Party, The Scottish Green Party, The Liberal Democrats & Scottish Socialist Party (p 34); Logos © National Farmers Union (Scotland), British Medical Association (Scotland), Greenpeace, Animal Liberation Front (public domain), Pedal on Parliament, The TaxPayers' Alliance & The Robin Hood Tax (p 36); Logos © UK Uncut & Greenpeace (p 37); Logos © Equity, Aslef & Unite (p 38); Logo © TUC/Image © Ljupco Smokovski/Shutterstock.com (p 38); Raul Mee/Creative Comons (CC BY-SA 2.0)[5] (p 40); UK Home Office (CC BY 2.0)[6] (p 41); Chris McAndrew/Creative Commons (CC BY-SA 3.0)[3] (p 41); JackWilfred/Creative Commons (CC BY-SA 4.0)[2] (p 41); Andrew Milligan/PA Archive/Press Association Images (p 41); Headline © The Scotsman Publications used with their kind permission (p 43); A headline from The Herald 21 April 2013 © Herald & Times Group (p 43); Logos © Twitter, Inc., Facebook, YouTube, LLC & Mumsnet Limited (p 43); Kovnir Andrii/Shutterstock.com (p 46); 1000 Words/Shutterstock.com (p 48); Monkey Business Images/Shutterstock.com (p 50); John Fleming/Creative Commons (CC BY-SA 3.0)[1] (p 56); shirokazan/Creative Commons (CC BY 2.0)[6] (p 56); BaLL LunLa/Shutterstock.com (p 57); vchal/Istockphotos (p 58); Image reproduced by permission of Big Partnership (p 59); Image reproduced by permission of Herald & Times Group (p 60); Andy Dean Photography/Shutterstock.com (p 62); Mega Pixel/Shutterstock.com (p 64); Domofon/Shutterstock.com (p 65); Graeme Maclean/Creative Commons (CC BY 2.0)[6] (p 66); Katie Chan/Creative Commons (CC BY-SA 4.0)[2] (p 67); I See Modern Britain/Creative Commons (CC BY 2.0)[6] (p 71); RonAlmog/Creative Commons (CC BY 2.0)[6] (p 74); Chris Upson/Creative Commons (CC BY-SA 2.0)[5] (p 76); Image © Jonathan Brady/PA Wire (p 77); Polmont Young Offenders Institution photo licensed under the Open Government Licence v2.0. (p 79); Flag of Brazil (public domain) (p 84); Beto Barata/PR/ Creative Commons (CC BY 2.0)[6] (p 84); Marco Gomes/Creative Commons (CC BY 2.0)[6] (p 86); Agência Brasil/Creative Commons (CC BY 3.0 BR)[7] (p 87); Neil Palmer/CIAT/Creative Commons (CC BY-SA 2.0)[5] (p 88); Flag of India (public domain) (p 90); dp Photography/Shutterstock.com (p 92); OlegD/Shutterstock.com (p 94); Agência Brasil/Creative Commons (CC BY 3.0 BR)[7] (p 94); Logos © The National Rifle Association of America & National Right to Life (p 97); Rakkhi Samarasekera/Creative Commons (CC BY 2.0)[6] (p 98); Kremlin.ru/Creative Commons (CC BY 4.0)[8] (p 102); Logo © United Nations (p 102); Logos © UNICEF, WHO, UNHCR, World Food Programme & United Nations Development Programme (p 103); Logo © Amnesty International (p 104); Petty Officer 2nd Class Ernesto Hernandez Fonte/DVIDSHUB/Creative Commons (CC BY 2.0)[6] (p 106); Grüne Bundestagsfraktion/Creative Commons (CC BY 2.0)[6] (p 107); U.S. Signal Corps (public domain) (p 111); Image from http://childrenandarmedforces.un.org/children-not-soldiers/ © United Nations. Reprinted with the permission of the United Nations (p 112); Logo © Child Soldiers International (p 112); Emoji One/Creative Commons (CC BY-SA 4.0)[2] (p 116); Philip Date/Shutterstock.com (p 117); © UNICEF/UN018992/Hakim George (p 119); Al MacDonald/Creative Commons (CC BY-SA 3.0)[3] (p 120); © UNICEF/UN067903/Gonzalez (p 121).

[1] (OGL v.3) http://www.nationalarchives.gov.uk/doc/open-government-licence/version/3/

[2] (CC BY-SA 4.0) http://creativecommons.org/licenses/by-sa/4.0/deed.en

[3] (CC BY-SA 3.0) http://creativecommons.org/licenses/by-sa/3.0/

[4] (CC BY-ND 2.0) http://creativecommons.org/licenses/by-nd/2.0/

[5] (CC BY-SA 2.0) http://creativecommons.org/licenses/by-sa/2.0/

[6] (CC BY 2.0) http://creativecommons.org/licenses/by/2.0/

[7] (CC BY 3.0 BR) http://creativecommons.org/licenses/by/3.0/br/deed.en

[8] (CC BY 4.0) https://creativecommons.org/licenses/by/4.0/deed.ast

Printed and bound in the UK by W&G Baird

CONTENTS

BRIGHTRED STUDY GUIDE: NATIONAL 5 MODERN STUDIES

DEMOCRACY IN SCOTLAND AND THE UK

SOCIAL ISSUES IN THE UNITED KINGDOM

INTERNATIONAL ISSUES

GLOSSARY

INTRODUCING NATIONAL 5 MODERN STUDIES

Political issues, like who has the power in a country or the decisions governments make, and social issues, like inequality and crime, exist in Scotland and all around the world. In the 21st century, the world we live in has never been more closely connected. Through the internet, 24-hour news channels and social media we are bombarded with information and opinion on all sort of issues.

Modern Studies aims to use the social sciences of politics, sociology, economics and others to help students make sense of these issues, and form well-thought-out and balanced opinions about them.

Knowing about these topics is not going to be enough when it comes to being successful in your future career; you also need to be able to communicate with others about what you know, sharing your information and opinion in a number of ways. National 5 aims to equip you with these skills as well as knowledge.

THE BENEFITS OF NATIONAL 5

National 5 Modern Studies is a course that allows you to develop an in-depth understanding of many of the most important and interesting issues in Scottish and/ or UK politics, UK society and in or between important countries or international organisations.

The course will equip you with a range of skills to help you be a confident individual and effective contributor in your further studies, your chosen career and your wider life. These include the skills of effective research, understanding and analysing a range of conflicting information, working with other people, and communicating/presenting what you know and understand.

THE EXTERNAL ASSESSMENT: COMPONENT 1 – QUESTION PAPER

The Course Assessment will be what decides your grade for National 5 Modern Studies. This course can be passed with a grade from the highest (A) down to a C. The Question Paper is worth 80 marks (80% of the total marks). Most of these marks are for knowledge and understanding, and the rest are for source-based skills questions.

You will have 2 hours and 20 minutes to complete the Question Paper.

The Question Paper will measure the breadth and application of your learning, and challenge you to show how much you understand the course.

Breadth, application and challenge

The Course Assessment will test your knowledge and understanding from the three units which you have studied:
- Democracy in Scotland and the United Kingdom
- Social Issues in the United Kingdom
- International Issues

Knowledge and understanding

Each section has a question with two optional parts, and in each option, you must answer four questions. Three questions will assess your knowledge and understanding and the fourth question will assess your evaluating skills.

contd

You should answer four questions in total. However, you must answer one question from each section

In each unit, you are expected to be able to give detailed descriptions and explanations and provide some alalysis.

Skills questions

In these questions you will be given sources of information, containing a mixture of words and numbers, and you must be able to:

- support and oppose a view using a limited range of sources of information (pages 44–45)
- make and justify a decision using a limited range of sources of information (pages 80–81)
- draw and support conclusions using a limited range of sources of information (pages 122–123).

For each of these types of question, you will need to give detailed descriptions and explanations, with some analysis.

THE EXTERNAL ASSESSMENT: COMPONENT 2 – ASSIGNMENT

The Assignment is worth 20 marks (20% of the total mark).

Unlike the Question Paper, the Assignment has more marks available for skills than knowledge and understanding.

You will have up to 1 hour to complete the Assignment.

The Assignment will ask you to: choose an appropriate Modern Studies topic or issue; collect evidence on this topic from at least two different types of source/research methods; discuss the strengths and weaknesses of these research methods, and how useful they are; apply your source-based skills to the collected evidence; explain and analyse the topic studied, using your Modern Studies knowledge and understanding; and reach a well-supported conclusion, with evidence, about the topic.

HOW WILL THIS GUIDE HELP YOU MEET THE CHALLENGES?

This guide is designed to give you the best possible chance to succeed in National 5 Modern Studies. Completing the course will not be easy, and you are expected to know a lot, but this book will give you a very strong foundation for achieving a great grade in the course.

Each section contains detailed examples and explanations of the relevant topic, in as user-friendly a way as possible.

Skills questions are approached in the designated spreads.

Throughout this book we promise we will at all times be talking to you and not at you!

Added to the work you complete in school and as homework, use of this book should put you in a really strong position to achieve your potential in National 5 Modern Studies.

ONLINE

This book is supported by the BrightRED Digital Zone - log on at www.brightredbooks.net/N5ModernStudies for a world of tests, activities, videos and more!

THE UK POLITICAL SYSTEM

LAYERS OF DECISION MAKING

The UK has layers of decision making. At different levels, different people and organisations make the decisions. Above all, the law in the UK decides what decisions can and cannot be made. Each new law must be officially approved by the monarch (the head of the Royal Family).

The UK Parliament makes decisions that affect the whole of the UK in some areas, known as **reserved matters** (see pages 10–17). The Scottish Parliament, since **devolution**, makes decisions on areas that affect Scotland alone.

Local matters are decided by local councils (see the 'Local councils' and 'Work of local councillors' sections).

FACT

Scottish Devolution Referendum 1997 results
I agree that there should be a Scottish Parliament: 73.4%
I agree that a Scottish Parliament should have tax-varying powers: 63.5%

DEVOLUTION

In 1997, the Labour Party won the UK **general election** and formed the UK Government. They had a **manifesto** promise to hold a **referendum** (a public vote over one decision) on giving Scotland a **parliament** of its own. The referendum passed, and the Scottish Parliament was set up in 1999.

Devolved and reserved matters

Devolved matters	Reserved matters
Agriculture, forestry and fisheries	Benefits and social security
Education and training	Immigration
Environment	Defence
Health and social services	Foreign policy
Housing	Employment
Law and order	Broadcasting
Local government	Trade and industry
Sport and the arts	Nuclear energy, oil, coal, gas and electricity
Tourism and economic development	Consumer rights
Transport	Data protection
	The Constitution

Devolved and reserved matters

The Scottish Parliament was set up to work alongside the UK Parliament in making decisions for Scotland. As such, the power to make laws only in certain areas, which affect only Scotland, was given over to the Scottish Parliament. These **policy** areas are called **devolved matters**, for example education is a devolved matter. This means Scotland can (and unusually has always been able to) create its own education policy. Only students in Scotland study National 5 qualifications, and Modern Studies in fact!

On the other hand, the UK Parliament retains the power to make laws about areas that affect the whole of the UK or have an international impact. These areas are called reserved matters.

THE FUTURE OF SCOTTISH DECISION MAKING

On the 1 May 2012, the UK Parliament passed the Scotland Act (2012). This Act allows the Scottish Parliament to set income tax rates in Scotland and borrow more money: a combined £5 billion in new financial powers. The UK Government described it as the biggest transfer of financial power to Scotland in 300 years.

Other powers, including the regulation of air guns, drink-driving, and speed limits, and a role in broadcasting, and taxes including stamp duty, land tax and landfill tax, will also be devolved. These new powers came into effect with the Scotland Act (2016), which also granted devolved powers on borrowing, welfare, transport, abortion, consumer advocacy, equal opportunities and gambling.

contd

Of course, if Scotland had voted 'Yes' to independence in the referendum of 18 September 2014 there would have been no more devolved and reserved matters: the Scottish Parliament would have made all of the decisions for Scotland. At this time, the Scottish National Party (SNP) Government commented that the Scotland Act 2012 may be 'bypassed by events'. However, this was not to be as when the people of Scotland were asked the question – should Scotland be an independent country? – 55.3% of them said 'no'.

	Votes	Percentage
Yes	1,617,989	44.7
No	2,001,926	55.3
Valid Votes	3,619,915	99.91
Invalid Votes	3,429	0.09
Total Votes	**3,623,344**	**100**

(Wikipedia)

As the Constitution is a reserved matter, the UK Government had to grant the Scottish Parliament unusual powers in order to hold a referendum, called a Section 30 agreement. The SNP Scottish Government had to negotiate with the UK Government about how and when the referendum would be run. On 15 October 2012, Prime Minister David Cameron and First Minister Alex Salmond signed the agreement on the Scottish referendum deal, which Alex Salmond called the Edinburgh Agreement.

PARLIAMENTS IN THE UK

The UK Parliament has evolved over more than 1000 years, going through many changes in that time. It has evolved to have two houses: the House of Commons and the House of Lords. A parliamentary system with two houses like this is called **bicameral**.

In each chamber, the government and **opposition** (the biggest party that is not in the government) sit on opposite benches, facing each other. This could be seen to encourage confrontation between the parties.

The Scottish Parliament is young in contrast, created new in 1999, with the Scottish Parliament building being completed in 2004. This allowed the Scottish Parliament to take the best parts of the UK system and change the ones that it thought it could do better. There is only one house in the Scottish Parliament, with no equivalent to the House of Lords. A parliamentary system with one house is called **unicameral**.

In the Scottish Parliament chamber the members of the Scottish Parliament (MSPs) sit in a semi-circular arrangement. This could be seen to encourage cooperation between the parties.

Parliament and government

The party (or parties in a **coalition**) that has the most members of parliament (MPs) or MSPs elected forms the **government**. This is the institution which runs the country and introduces the most Bills in the country.

The leader of the winning party in the UK becomes the Prime Minister and is officially asked by the Queen to form the government. In Scotland, however, the First Minister is elected from amongst the MSPs after each Scottish election.

The **Cabinet** is the central group of government members. It coordinates the work of different government departments and decides government policy. The UK Cabinet has about 20 members, while the Scottish Cabinet has around 10 members.

Cabinet meetings happen in private and individual members must support the decisions that the Cabinet makes. This is called **collective responsibility**.

VIDEO LINK

Check out the clip about the House of Commons chamber at www.brightredbooks.net/N5ModernStudies.

VIDEO LINK

Check out the clip about the House of Lords chamber at www.brightredbooks.net/N5ModernStudies.

VIDEO LINK

Watch the video 'The Scottish Parliament' at www.brightredbooks.net/N5ModernStudies.

ONLINE TEST

Test yourself on the UK political system online at www.brightredbooks.net/N5ModernStudies.

THINGS TO DO AND THINK ABOUT

1 Make a spider diagram of devolved and reserved matters.

2 'The Scottish Parliament makes most of the important decisions for Scotland.'

    Do you agree with this statement? Give reasons for your answer.

3 Explain what each of the following terms means in your own words:

    • referendum   • government   • Cabinet

4 Find out the name and role of a member of the Scottish or UK Cabinet.

YOUR REPRESENTATIVES

THE NATURE OF REPRESENTATION

Levels of decision making.

Type of issue	Decisions made by	Your representative(s)
Local	Local authority/council	Local councillors (three or four)
Scottish	Scottish Parliament	Constituency MSP Regional MSPs (seven)
National (UK)	UK Parliament	Constituency MP
European	European Parliament	Scotland's MEPs (six)

Each of us is represented by a number of different people, at a number of different levels of decision making. From local councils right up to the European Parliament in Brussels there are people whose job it is to speak up for us and our interests.

DON'T FORGET

At all levels it is the job of representatives to speak on behalf of their constituents.

POLITICAL PARTIES IN THE UK

Most representatives at each level stand for election as members of a political party. Each political party changes its policies in line with circumstances to try and give themselves the best chance to be elected. However, parties do have different **ideologies**: sets of beliefs about how to make Scotland or the UK better. The summaries below are based on the 2017 general election and 2016 Scottish election (SNP) manifestos.

Conservative
- Corporation tax to fall to 17% by 2020.
- Defence spending would increase by 0.5% more than inflation each year.
- A vote would be held on repealing the fox hunting ban.
- £4 billion to be spent on schools by 2022.
- Migrant workers would face higher NHS charges.

Labour
- No increase to VAT or National Insurance Contributions.
- Abolish the Bedroom Tax.
- Pension age frozen at 66 from 2020.
- Free childcare (30 hours) extended to all two-year-olds.
- Free lunches for school pupils as part of a £6 million package.

Liberal Democrat
- Referendum on the Brexit deal with an option to remain in the EU.
- Lifting of the 1% cap on public sector pay.
- Introduction of a legal and regulated market for cannabis.
- £6 billion for NHS, social care services and public health.
- A 'rent-to-own' scheme for young people.

SNP
- A new Climate Change Act.
- 50,000 new homes will be built.
- £20 billion infrastructure programme.
- Faster broadband throughout Scotland.
- More training places for GPs and advance nurse practitioners.

There are also a number of minor parties, like the Greens, UKIP (United Kingdom Independence Party) and the BNP, who have different ideologies.

CONTACTING YOUR REPRESENTATIVES

Once elected, an MP or MSP's job is one which involves frequent communication. In order to be able to represent the interests of his/her **constituents** (the people they represent), each representative must be able to hear from them. They provide a number of ways in which to do this. On the official website of the organisation, and their own website,

contd

you will be able to find an e-mail address and/or telephone number for the representative. At least from Scottish Parliament level upwards, representatives have **constituency** offices, which you can visit or contact to raise concerns or issues with that representative.

Increasingly, representatives are turning to social media to have instant communication with their constituents. For example, Ian Murray, MP for Edinburgh South, actively uses Twitter (@IanMurrayMP) to get in touch with his constituents and keep them up to date with his work on their behalf.

May 2018 – Ian Murray supporting Young Cardiac Arrest

THE WORK OF MPs AND MSPs IN CONSTITUENCIES

As well as having to be easy to contact by concerned or interested constituents, MPs and MSPs have a great deal of work to do in their constituencies.

MPs and MSPs hold **surgeries** in their constituencies. These are scheduled times when any concerned constituent can come and speak face to face with their representative. Details of when surgeries are to take place will appear on the representative's website and perhaps in the local newspaper. Surgeries allow the representative to hear about the problems or issues their constituents face. The representative can tell the constituent about any work that is already being done on the matter or can take the problem up with the relevant people involved, perhaps in parliament.

MSPs and MPs also often attend social events in their constituencies. This shows an active interest in the people and place they represent. It also allows constituents to informally get to know their representative(s) and see them as more approachable if they do have a problem in the future. Ian Murray MP attended the St Peter's PTA Fair Duck Race in 2018.

Representatives also go on fact-finding missions to schools, businesses and other organisations in their constituencies. This helps the representative hear about how things are going in their area from the people who are directly involved. This also gives constituents the chance to ask a representative face to face about any issues they're having and what the representative plans to do about it.

On visits to schools, the pupils – constituents who are nearly all too young to vote – get a chance to put really probing questions to their representative. On a visit to Craigour Park Primary School in May 2018, pupils told Ian Murray MP about their efforts to reduce plastic and paper use in the school.

When constituents have raised a concern with their MP or MSP about something that involves a business or other organisation, the MP or MSP may meet with the organisation or organisations involved. By doing this, they hope to find a solution for their constituents that the constituents may not have managed to achieve themselves. Tavish Scott, MSP for Shetland, raised concerns about Shetland being 'put in a box' on maps. He told the Rural Economy and Connectivity Committee that the islands should not be misrepresented and should be in the right place on the map, a statement that Humza Yousaf, then Transport and the Islands Minister agreed with. In June 2018 Yousaf was promoted to Cabinet Secretary for Justice in Nicola Sturgeon's cabinet reshuffle.

ONLINE

Follow the link at www. brightredbooks.net/ N5ModernStudies to find Ian Murray on Twitter.

ONLINE TEST

Test yourself on your representatives online at www.brightredbooks.net/ N5ModernStudies.

THINGS TO DO AND THINK ABOUT

1   Use their websites to find out about the policies and ideologies of the Green Party or UKIP.

2   Search online for the most up-to-date party manifestos and compare policies in a policy area not shown above.

3   Use the Internet to find out who your elected representatives are (MP and MSP).

Look at their parliamentary and constituency websites to find examples of your MP or MSP working in any of the ways described above in your constituency.

MPs IN PARLIAMENT

VIDEO LINK

Have a look at this emergency debate from 2018 discussing the UK Government's approach to the humanitarian crisis in Syria at www.brightredbooks.net/N5ModernStudies. Labour MP Alison McGovern asked for the debate, so she gets to make the opening statement.

THE WORK OF MPs

The UK Parliament meets at Westminster, London. The main tasks of parliament are to make new laws, and debate and discuss how to make the UK a better place to live.

Concerned citizens may feel an issue is important enough to be brought publicly to their MP's attention. They have the right to go to parliament and tell the MP directly about it. This is called **lobbying**, as they are allowed to approach MPs in the lobby of parliament with these concerns. Lobbying groups or individuals can get a lot of media attention for their cause.

In a typical week MPs meet in the House of Commons from Monday afternoon until Friday afternoon.

It is the main job of MPs to represent their constituents in the House of Commons. This means that MPs can raise the concerns of their constituents and speak up for their points of view. MPs can do this in a number of ways.

DEBATES

Debates are an opportunity for MPs to discuss government policy and current issues, and propose new laws. They allow MPs to voice the concerns and interests of their constituents. They also give MPs a chance to hear different opinions and reach a more balanced point of view.

Debates often get 'lively', so someone has to take charge. In the UK Parliament this person is called the Speaker.

General debates	Adjournment debates	Emergency debates
A general debate is held on a proposal (**motion**) put forward by an MP. These debates have strict rules, enforced by the Speaker. Decisions at the end of a general debate are made by a 'division' (vote).	These are general debates that MPs do not have to vote on. They allow backbench MPs the chance to bring their constituents' concerns to the attention of the House. There is a half-hour debate at the end of each day's sitting.	When a serious issue catches an MP's attention, they can ask the Speaker to grant an emergency debate in which MPs can discuss the issue. The Speaker rarely grants these.

DIVISIONS (VOTES)

When a **division** is called by the Speaker, the division bell rings throughout parliament (and in two pubs nearby!) to call MPs to vote: they have 8 minutes to get to the chamber and vote.

MPs vote by leaving the Commons chamber and going to either the 'Aye' (yes) lobby or the 'No' lobby. Their vote is officially counted as they re-enter the chamber.

Before deciding which way to vote, MPs have to balance what their constituents think, their party's policy and their own opinion. These points of view may be very different!

This is the division bell in St Stephen's Tavern next to the Palace of Westminster.

QUESTION TIME

Question Time takes place every Monday to Thursday for an hour. It gives MPs a chance to ask government ministers about any issues that are their responsibility. For example, if an MP had a question about the military, they could ask the Defence Secretary.

contd

MPs must submit their questions in advance, but can ask a supplementary (extra, follow-on) question after the minister has answered.

Prime Minister's Question Time

Prime Minister's Question Time (PMQs) takes place from 12 noon to 12:30pm every Wednesday when parliament is in session. PMQs always starts with the open question: Question 1: *'If the Prime Minister has any engagements for the rest of the day.'* Following the answer, the MP then asks their supplementary question about an issue they or their constituents feel is important.

The Leader of the Opposition then follows up on this or another topic. They are permitted to ask a total of six questions. The Leader of the Opposition is the only MP who is allowed to come back with further questions.

In theory, the Prime Minister will not know what supplementary questions will be asked of them. However, the Prime Minister will be prepared for likely questions by government departments.

ONLINE

Visit 'BBC Parliament' on BBC iPlayer (www.brightredbooks. net/N5ModernStudies) to find a recent example of Prime Minister's Questions. What sort of issues are being discussed?

COMMITTEES

In the Houses of Parliament much of the work is done in committees. It is the main job of the committees to scrutinise (keep a close eye on) how the government is doing. Committees are made up of 10–50 MPs (and Lords in some cases) from more than one of the parties in parliament.

General Committees consider Bills (proposed laws) and come up with any changes they think should be made to them. A General Committee can have between 16 and about 50 members, of which the government always has a majority. The committee will call in expert witnesses to give their opinions or receive their opinions in writing. This is called the committee stage (see pages 16–17).

Select Committees hold inquiries in which they investigate issues that they think are important to the British public. Each Select Committee works on topics relating to a specific government department, e.g. the Defence Committee. Committees can call people to give evidence and to face questions from the committee's members.

Examples of Select Committee membership (September 2017)	
Committee	*Defence*
Total members	11
Conservative	Dr Julian Lewis (Chair) Leo Docherty Mark Francois Johnny Mercer
Labour	Graham P Jones Madeleine Moon Ruth Smeeth John Spellar Phil Wilson
Scottish National Party	Martin Docherty-Hughes
Democratic Unionist Party	Gavin Robinson

Grand Committees give MPs the chance to debate issues affecting their regions. These committees work like the House of Commons chamber, with statements from government ministers and a chance to ask them questions. There is a Grand Committee each for Scotland, Wales and Northern Ireland, and eight Grand Committees for English regions. The Scottish Grand Committee has not met for a number of years, as there have been few Bills affecting only Scotland since the formation of the Scottish Parliament.

MPs can represent their constituents by joining committees that deal with issues their constituents are likely to be interested in.

PRIVATE MEMBERS' BILLS

An MP who is not a government minister can also attempt to make a new law by introducing a **Private Member's Bill**. These are rarely passed, as there is not much of parliament's time to devote to them. However, even if the Bill doesn't get passed by parliament, it can bring attention to the issue.

ONLINE TEST

Take the test on MPs in parliament online at www.brightredbooks.net/ N5ModernStudies.

THINGS TO DO AND THINK ABOUT

1 Use the UK Parliament's 'Find Your MP' tool (http://findyourmp.parliament.uk/) to find out who your MP is. Look at their parliamentary and constituency websites to find examples of your MP working to represent you in parliament.

THE HOUSE OF LORDS

MEMBERS OF THE HOUSE OF LORDS

The House of Lords is the second chamber of the UK Parliament. It plays a crucial role in making and shaping laws, and keeping a close eye on the UK Government.

There are around 800 members of the House of Lords. Unlike MPs in the House of Commons, **peers** are not elected by the public. There are three types of members, or peers, in the Lords.

Appointed Peers	
Baroness Grey-Thompson	Former Paralympian
Lord Sugar	Businessman
Baroness Mone	Businesswoman
(Elected) Hereditary Peers	
Lord Borwick	Elected July 2013
Viscount Ridley	Elected February 2013
Bishops	
Justin Welby	Archbishop of Canterbury

Life peers

Most members of the Lords are life peers, appointed by the Queen. They are recommended by an independent organisation called the Appointments Commission. The Appointments Commission selects people to become peers because of their expertise, knowledge and experience in a specific area, such as science or business. The Commission also tries to 'ensure that the House of Lords represents the diversity of the people of the UK'.

(Elected) hereditary peers

For hundreds of years, the Lords was dominated by hereditary peers. These were peers who inherited their title from a parent, who in turn had inherited it from their parents: the title was passed from generation to generation.

However, this changed in 1999, and the Lords themselves had to vote on which 92 hereditary peers to keep. The rest lost their peerages. When these elected hereditary members pass away or leave the house, the other Lords will vote for another former hereditary peer to replace them. Hereditary peers have become another type of life peer.

Church of England bishops

The third type of peer is made up of 26 bishops from the Church of England. The Archbishop of Canterbury is the most famous of these. The bishops keep their peerage as long as they stay in their position: if they retire or leave the church, their peerage passes on.

There are peers of many different religions in the House of Lords, but the Church of England is the only one that has official representation.

GROUPS OF LORDS

Peers sit in four different groups: government, opposition, **cross-benchers** and bishops. Government peers are peers that are members of whatever party or parties make up the government at that time. Opposition peers are peers who are members of any other parties.

Cross-benchers are peers who were appointed because of their expertise or experience, and don't belong to any party. The bishops aren't members of a party either. As there are so many cross-benchers, the government nearly always has a minority of peers.

The person who is in charge of the running of the House of Lords is called the Lord Speaker. Unlike the Speaker of the House of Commons, the Lord Speaker cannot ask members to be quiet, instead the Lords is self-regulating (the peers look after themselves).

Instead of having a grand chair like in the House of Commons, the Lord Speaker sits on a big cushion-like chair called the woolsack.

The woolsack

ROLES OF THE HOUSE OF LORDS

The House of Lords is independent of the House of Commons, but the two chambers work together to make, pass and shape the laws that affect the whole of the UK. The Lords has three main roles: making laws, considering laws and holding government to account.

Making laws

Members of the House of Lords can introduce Private Members' Bills in the same way that MPs can. If the Bill is supported by an MP, it continues in the Commons (see pages 16–17). Similarly to MPs' Private Members' Bills, it is highly unlikely that Private Members' Bills from the Lords will be granted much time in the Commons.

Considering laws

Around half of the time in the House of Lords is spent considering Bills. The House of Commons and the Lords have to examine every Bill before it can become a law. The Lords plays a crucial role in this process because it allows peers – who do not have to worry about re-election every few years – to add their expert opinion to the law-making process (see pages 16–17). As peerages last a lifetime, the Lords can take a long-term view of any law that is being examined.

Peers may also join Select Committees and help investigate proposed new laws.

Scrutinising government

Members of the Lords play a vital role making laws and keeping a check on (scrutinising) what the UK Government does. They can do this in two main ways: Question Time and debates.

There is a 30-minute question time at the start of business from Monday to Thursday. Peers can ask a government spokesperson up to four initial questions, and then supplementary questions, in each of these. Lords can also submit questions to the government in writing.

In debates, peers add their considerable experience to the discussion of government proposals.

FACT

Since the Parliament Act 1949 came into force the Lords cannot amend or delay Money Bills (Bills about taxes or public money). Money Bills will receive **Royal Assent** even if the Lords doesn't pass them.

FACT

Members of the Lords submit about 10,000 written questions to the government annually.

ONLINE TEST

Take the test on the House of Lords online at www.brightredbooks.net/N5ModernStudies.

THINGS TO DO AND THINK ABOUT

1   Use the House of Lords website (http://www.parliament.uk/business/lords/) to make a factfile about a peer:
    - What sort of peer are they (life, elected hereditary, bishop)?
    - When did they join the Lords?
    - What group do they belong to (government, opposition, cross-bench)?
    - What expertise or experience do they add to the Lords?

2   Use the House of Lords website (http://www.parliament.uk/mps-lords-and-offices/lords/composition-of-the-lords/) to find out the current number, types and parties of peers in the House of Lords.

3   Who do you think should be made a peer? Write a letter to the Appointments Commission, recommending someone for a peerage:
    - What skills or expertise would they add to the Lords?
    - Why are they the best person that the Appointments Commission could consider?

LORDS REFORM?

ARGUMENTS FOR AND AGAINST REFORM

The House of Lords is an extremely controversial part of the UK Parliamentary system. Many people see it as very important that before laws are made, another group of people can give a second opinion on them and that the government's decisions are closely scrutinised.

Many people, however, believe that having a second chamber that is unelected – that the public haven't voted for – is against the principles of **democracy**. These people believe that the House of Lords should either be abolished (got rid of completely) or reformed (changed).

Pros and cons of the current House of Lords

Pros	Cons
Many peers are now extremely experienced in the workings of parliament: to change the system would lose all this expertise.	Important decisions are being made by unelected people who don't have to answer to the public for their decisions through elections.
Not having to worry about re-election, peers can make difficult decisions that may be unpopular in the short term in the long-term interests of the country.	Public opinion should be at the centre of all decisions taken by those in power: it is undemocratic if this is ignored or not taken into account by the Lords.
As it is appointed to give a second opinion, it is clear that the Commons is the main decision-making House. Electing the Lords would make this difference unclear.	The Lords votes on nearly all Bills (proposed laws), and such an important function should be left to those who are chosen by the people.
The Appointments Commission is independent and picks the best people for the job; the public may just choose a popular personality if they were voting.	Voters should be able to choose whomever they like to make decisions on their behalf in parliament.
It's worked for a very long time: why change it now?	The Lords has blocked Bills that the public support: maybe it's not working in the public interest?

The Electoral Reform Society – an organisation that wants to change the UK voting and parliamentary systems – says: 'If you hold the power to help decide how Britain is run you should be elected by us, the British public. That's democracy.' They also claim that 79% of the public support reform.

VIEWS ON THE HOUSE OF LORDS

Many individuals, such as Terry Burns, former permanent secretary to the treasury, believe that the House of Lords is swelling, and action must be taken to reduce the number of peers. Currently, in 2018, there are 826 peers in the upper chamber. Terry proposes a 'one in two out' policy and a number of other measures including implementing a 15-year term limit and ensuring one fifth of peerages are reserved for independent cross-benchers.

LORDS REFORM SINCE 2010

2010: The coalition agreement

After the 2010 general election, because no party won more than half of all seats in the House of Commons, the Conservative Party joined (formed a coalition) with the Liberal Democrats, to allow the two parties to form a coalition government.

Before this happened, the two parties negotiated and signed a coalition agreement that set out how they would work together, and what they would work towards. This document promised to 'establish a committee to bring forward proposals for a wholly or mainly elected upper chamber on the basis of **proportional representation**.

The House of Lords Reform Bill

2012

The coalition introduced the House of Lords Reform Bill. It proposed that the House of Lords should eventually consist of:

- 360 elected members (elected in batches of 120 every 5 years, with a 15-year term and no re-election)
- 90 appointed members
- up to 12 Lords Spiritual (bishops from the Church of England), and
- any ministerial members (of the government).

This would mean a House of Lords approximately half the size of the current House.

Two weeks later, the House of Commons had a vote on the second reading of the Bill (see the section 'Making laws in the UK'). The result was 462 votes to 124 in favour of continuing with the Bill. However, the result hid the biggest coalition **rebellion** up to that point: 91 Conservative MPs voted against their own coalition government's plan.

The Bill also only passed this stage when a programme motion, which allotted it time to pass through the House of Commons, was dropped. It was likely that the Bill would have been defeated (lost the vote) if it had contained a programme motion. This was also to give the Conservatives time to persuade their MPs of the benefits of reform.

Liberal Democrat leader Nick Clegg announced that the reform plans would be abandoned, instead of facing a 'slow death' in the House of Commons. He also said the Conservatives 'broke the coalition contract'. In response, he would tell Liberal Democrat MPs to vote against changes to constituency boundaries, which the Conservatives hoped to have in place before the 2015 election.

2017

In 2017, Labour leader Jeremy Corbyn stated that he would like his party's 2020 manifesto to include specific detail about the Labour Party's proposals for Lords reform. In a TV interview, Corbyn stated, *'We have a House of Lords which is dominated by a small number of people from London and the south east. I would want to see an elected second chamber that it is representative of all regions and nations of the United Kingdom. I think that's very, very important. I think it should have an electoral mandate to go with it.'*

ONLINE TEST

Take the 'Lords reform?' test online at www. brightredbooks.net/ N5ModernStudies.

THINGS TO DO AND THINK ABOUT

1   According to Jeremy Corbyn, the House of Lords is 'dominated by a small number of people from London and the south east', Why do you think this is the case?

2   Imagine you are a political adviser to the UK Government. You have been asked to write a report about the future of the Lords:

   a   Should it remain as it is, be reformed or be abolished?

   b   Who should be peers and why? Give at least three examples of current or prospective peers.

   c   Why do you think this is the best way forward?

   d   Link this back to the policies of each party to make your proposal as appealing as possible to all parties.

MAKING LAWS IN THE UK

THE ROLE OF WESTMINSTER

The UK Parliament makes all laws for England and laws for the whole UK about reserved matters. Introducing **legislation** (laws) also gives individual MPs, or groups of MPs, the chance to represent their constituents' concerns: trying to pass laws about issues that concern them. The first step in making a new law is to propose a **Bill**: a draft law.

TYPES OF BILLS

There are a number of different types of Bills, each given a different name depending on who introduced it. Some of these are given below.

Public Bills

Public Bills change the laws that affect every member of the public in the general population. These are the most common type of Bill. These are normally introduced by government ministers, but sometimes by other MPs or Lords, when they are known as Private Members' Bills.

Private Members' Bills

For an MP who is not in the government to introduce a Private Member's Bill, the MP must do one of three things. First, the ballot is a system in which all MPs applying for a Bill are drawn at random at the start of the parliamentary year. Usually, the first seven selected are timetabled to get a day's debate each. Because they are guaranteed this time, these Bills have the best chance of becoming law.

Second, there is the 10-minute rule. This gives MPs the chance to speak about an issue for up to 10 minutes. This gives MPs the opportunity of seeing if their idea for a Bill would have much support in the Commons.

Finally, there is presentation. Any MP can introduce a Bill into parliament as long as they have officially told the Speaker that they will do so. They are not given the chance to speak in support of their Bill, so these Bills very rarely become law.

Private Bills

Private Bills are Bills that only affect certain organisations, and are for when the organisation is requesting powers that are not the same as the law gives them already. For example, the City of London Corporation (Open Spaces) Act 2018 allows the Corporation to protect London's green space, issue Fixed Penalty Notices to those individuals who engage in anti-social behaviour and generate commercial income which can be reinvested for the greater good.

Hybrid Bills

Hybrid Bills are Bills that affect the whole population, but have a very significant impact on a specific area of the country, or a specific part of the population, or a specific group. The Bills that were passed to allow the Channel Tunnel to be built are examples of Hybrid Bills.

THE LEGISLATIVE PROCESS

There are a number of stages that a Bill must pass through before it can become a law. Bills beginning in the House of Commons must go through five stages in the Commons before repeating these stages in the Lords. Bills starting in the House of Lords do this in the opposite direction. There is then the consideration of amendments before Royal Assent can be granted, which makes the Bill into an **Act** (law).

DON'T FORGET

Introducing a Bill gives MPs a chance to represent their constituents by highlighting an issue of particular concern to them.

DON'T FORGET

Each Bill must go through multiple stages, in both Houses (Commons and Lords), before it can become a law.

Acts of the UK Parliament, 2011–2017.

25 23 33 30 37 25 35
2011 2012 2013 2014 2015 2016 2017

contd

First reading	The first reading is when the short title of the Bill is read out and its formal place in parliament's timetable is confirmed. There is no debate or discussion.
Second reading	This is also called the debate on the general principles of the Bill. At this stage, the MP responsible for the Bill speaks about why it is needed. Someone from the official Opposition then speaks about the Bill before backbench MPs and other opposition can have their say on it. After they have debated the Bill MPs vote on whether it should continue through parliament.
Committee stage	At this stage, the Bill is examined in detail by a committee of MPs (see page 11). The committee may take evidence from experts and interested groups from outside parliament. The committee may make changes (amendments) to the Bill if members of the committee vote to do so. Every clause (section) in the Bill is agreed to, changed or removed from the Bill by the committee.
Report stage	The report stage of a Bill is when all MPs are given the opportunity to consider making further amendments to it after it has been examined in committee. All MPs may speak and vote on the Bill at this stage or propose amendments. This all takes place in the debating chamber of the House of Commons.
Third reading	This is the last chance for the House of Commons to debate the contents of a Bill. A short debate is had, in which each section of the Bill can be included or not. After this debate, the Commons votes on whether or not to approve the third reading of the Bill.
The other House	After passing the third reading, the Bill is passed to the other House. Bills which started in the House of Commons pass to the House of Lords, and vice versa. The other House then proceeds with all the same stages up to this point.
Consideration of amendments	After both Houses have passed the Bill through its third reading, the Bill returns to the House it came from, with any amendments made by the other House. Before the Bill can pass this stage, both Houses have to agree on the exact wording of the Bill. This can cause the Bill to 'ping pong' between the Houses while amendments are agreed upon. On very rare occasions, where the Houses cannot agree on amendments, the Bill fails.
Royal Assent	This is the final stage, where the monarch agrees to make the Bill an Act (law). It is now a formality: it happens automatically.

So far, in 2018, there have been 14 bills which have passed through the full legislative process and became Acts of Parliament:

- Smart Meters Act 2018
- Sanctions and Anti-Money Laundering Act 2018
- Data Protection Act 2018
- Secure Tenancies (Victims of Domestic Abuse) Act 2018
- Financial Guidance and Claims Act 2018
- Laser Misuse (Vehicles) Act 2018
- Northern Ireland Budget (Anticipation and Adjustments) Act 2018
- Northern Ireland Assembly Members (Pay) Act 2018.
- Northern Ireland (Regional Rates and Energy) Act 2018
- Space Industry Act 2018
- Supply and Appropriation (Anticipation and Adjustments (Act) 2018
- Finance Act 2018
- Armed Forces (Flexible Working) Act 2018
- Telecommunications Infrastructure (Relief from Non-Domestic Rates) Act 2018.

FACT

Royal Assent was last refused in 1707, when Queen Anne refused a Bill on settling the militia in Scotland.

VIDEO LINK

Watch the video from the UK Parliament website which explains the whole process at www.brightredbooks.net/N5ModernStudies.

ONLINE TEST

Take the UK legislative process test online at www.brightredbooks.net/N5ModernStudies.

THINGS TO DO AND THINK ABOUT

1. Research and makes notes on a Bill the UK Parliament is looking at just now, using the UK Parliament's 'Bills before Parliament' page: http://services.parliament.uk/bills/.

    a. What type of Bill is it? Who introduced it?

    b. What does it hope to achieve?

    c. What stage is it at?

2. Do the same for a recent Act of the UK Parliament (see http://www.parliament.uk/business/bills-and-legislation/current-bills/previous-bills/).

    a. Present the Act to the class.

ONLINE

Head to the BrightRED Digital Zone for a great activity about Passing a Private Members' Bill!

MSPs IN PARLIAMENT 1

THE WORK OF MSPs

The Scottish Parliament meets in Edinburgh to make decisions about devolved matters. The main tasks of the Scottish Parliament are to make new laws, and debate and discuss how to make Scotland a better place to live.

MSPs are usually in parliament for at least three days of the week: Tuesdays, Wednesdays and Thursdays. Parliament is in session (meets) for around 35 weeks per year. When it is not meeting, parliament is in recess.

Concerned citizens may feel an issue is important enough to be brought publicly to their MSP's attention. They have the right to go to parliament and tell the MSP directly about it. This is called lobbying, as they are allowed to approach MSPs in the lobby of parliament with these concerns. Lobbying groups or individuals can get a lot of media attention for their cause.

An MSP's main job is to represent their constituents in the Scottish Parliament. This means that MSPs can raise the concerns of the constituents and speak up for their point of view. MSPs can do this in a number of ways.

DEBATES

Debates are an opportunity for MSPs to discuss government policy and current issues, and propose new laws. MSPs can put forward motions about problems their constituents have raised and can ask parliament to consider how to solve them.

They also give MSPs a chance to hear different opinions and reach a more balanced point of view.

Debates often get 'lively', so someone has to take charge. In the Scottish Parliament, this person is called the **Presiding Officer**. He/she is an elected MSP who is voted in to

contd

this important and impartial role by the other MSPs. In May 2016, Ken Macintosh was elected to the role of presiding officer.

General debates

General debates are plenary (summing up) debates held on a proposal (**motion**) put forward by an MSP, usually a minister or Cabinet secretary.

These debates have strict rules, and it is the Presiding Officer's job to enforce these. At the start of the debate, the Presiding Officer says: 'Members who wish to take part in the debate should press the Request to Speak button now.' This allows the Presiding Officer to work out (and remind the MSPs) how much time each MSP can speak for in the debate.

General debates give MSPs a chance to represent their constituents by making points that reflect their point of view. There are not always votes at the end of a general debate.

Members' business debates

Members' business debates are an opportunity for an MSP to represent their constituents by raising a local issue or bringing up a certain event to which the Scottish Parliament may not otherwise devote time to discuss. Only MSPs who are not a Cabinet secretary or minister are allowed to propose motions during members' business debates. For example, on 24th January 2018, Gail Ross, MSP for Caithness, Sutherland and Ross, introduced a motion on 'Adverse Childhood Experiences' in a members' business debate.

These debates happen after Decision Time on Wednesdays and Thursdays, and last for up to 45 minutes.

Emergency debates

When a serious issue comes to the Presiding Officer's attention, he/she can grant an emergency debate in which MSPs can discuss the issue. These are rarely granted.

In August 2009, the Presiding Officer granted an emergency debate so that the Cabinet Secretary for Justice, Kenny MacAskill, could issue a statement and answer questions about his decision to release the convicted Lockerbie bomber Abdelbaset Ali Mohmed al-Megrahi. In his opening statement, the Presiding Officer said: 'This topic is of the utmost seriousness, and the eyes of many people around the globe are on the parliament today.'

DIVISIONS (VOTES)

When the parliament must make a decision, for example about a Bill, a division is called by the Presiding Officer. Most of the divisions are held at **Decision Time**, at 5pm on Tuesdays to Thursdays, and 12 noon on Fridays.

A division bell rings throughout the parliament to tell MSPs to go to the chamber to vote. In the Scottish Parliament, MSPs vote by pressing a button on their electronic consoles. There are three voting options: 'Yes', 'No' and 'Abstain' (choose not to vote).

Before deciding which way to vote, MSPs have to balance what their constituents think, their party's policy and their own opinion. These points of view may be very different!

Scottish Parliament voting console.

ONLINE TEST

Take the MSPs in parliament test online at www.brightredbooks.net/N5ModernStudies.

MSPs IN PARLIAMENT 2

QUESTION TIME

There are different forms of Question Time which take place in the Scottish Parliament. MSPs are given the opportunity to ask questions that are of great interest to them or to represent their constituents by asking questions about an issue that concerns them.

First Minister's Question Time

First Minister's Question Time (FMQs) takes place for half an hour every week, usually on Thursdays at noon. The other MSPs, in particular the leaders of the opposition parties, have the chance to ask the First Minister questions about decisions that the government has made or plans to make.

FMQs is where it is possible to see MSPs at their most rowdy and badly behaved: shouting over each other and making cheeky remarks. The Presiding Officer is required to keep the peace!

FMQs starts with the open question: *'To ask the First Minister what engagements she has planned for the rest of the day.'* Following the answer, the MSP then asks their real question about a current issue.

The Leader of the Opposition then follows up on this or another topic. The other parties are allocated questions according to their share of MSPs in the parliament.

In theory, the First Minister will not know what questions will be asked. However, the First Minister will be prepared for likely questions by government departments.

Topical Question Time

This normally takes place on a Tuesday and allows MSPs to ask questions about issues that have very recently happened, but that parliament hasn't discussed yet.

Portfolio (General) Question Time

Portfolio Question Time is when MSPs are given the chance to ask Cabinet secretaries and ministers questions about the policy area they are responsible for. For example, MSPs can ask the Minister for Public Health questions about health and wellbeing in Scotland.

This usually takes place on a Wednesday, for around half an hour.

VIDEO LINK

Watch the latest FMQs at www.brightredbooks.net/N5ModernStudies.

COMMITTEES

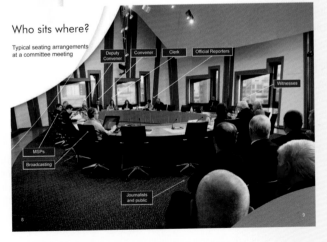

Who sits where?

Typical seating arrangements at a committee meeting

Deputy Convener · Convener · Clerk · Official Reporters · Witnesses · MSPs · Broadcasting · Journalists and public

Committees play a vital role in the work of the Scottish Parliament. The Scottish Parliament is unicameral (has only one house or level, without the equivalent of the House of Lords in the UK Parliament), so the committees are even more important than they are in the UK Parliament.

The Scottish Parliament has different types of committee (mandatory and subject) and can form new ones if specific issues or Bills need to be considered. Each committee is involved in a certain policy area or areas.

contd

Mandatory committees are committees that must exist in every session of the Scottish Parliament (between each Scottish Parliament election). These cover topics such as European and external relations, finance and public petitions.

Subject committees are formed at the start of, or during, a session (after each Scottish Parliament election) and are formed to look at a group of policy or subject areas until the next election. Examples include the Education and Skills Committee and the Jusitice Committee.

The membership of committees is usually between 5 and 15 members, and is supposed to roughly reflect the balance of parties in parliament: the more MSPs a party has the more MSPs it should have in each committee.

Selected committees and membership		
Committee	Equal Opportunities Committee	Referendum Bill Committee
Type	Mandatory	Subject
Membership	5	11
SNP	Angus MacDonald (Deputy Convener) Rona Mackay	James Dornah (Convener) George Adam Richard Lochhead Gordon MacDonald Gillian Maetin
Labour	Johann Lamont (Convener)	Johann Lamont (Deputy Convener) Mary Fee
Conservative	Rachael Hamilton Brian Whittle	Oliver Mundell Liz Smith
Liberal Democrat		Tavish Scott
Green		Ross Greer

Committees usually meet once a week or fortnightly, on a Tuesday, Wednesday or Thursday morning. These meetings are held in public so that journalists and ordinary citizens can see what discussions the committees are having.

Committees are heavily involved in scrutinising (investigating closely) the laws that government or MSPs want to make (see pages 22–23), and do this to make sure that the decisions made are the best possible results for Scotland. One way they can do this by inviting witnesses (including Cabinet secretaries and ministers) to speak and answer questions about the issues being examined. Committees also go on fact-finding missions to the areas affected to gather first-hand evidence.

PRIVATE MEMBERS' BILLS

Any MSP who is not a member of the government can also try to introduce a Member's Bill to parliament (see pages 22–23). This Bill could be about an issue that constituents feel strongly about or that affects the area the MSP represents.

ONLINE TEST

Take the MSPs in parliament test online at www.brightredbooks.net/N5ModernStudies.

THINGS TO DO AND THINK ABOUT

Use the Scottish Parliament's 'Find Your MSP' tool (http://www.parliament.scot/mspfinder/index.html) to find out who your MSP is. Look at their parliamentary and constituency websites to find examples of your MSP working to represent you in all different ways.

MAKING LAWS IN SCOTLAND

The Scottish Parliament passes laws about devolved matters when MSPs feel that a law will make Scotland a better place. Introducing legislation (laws) also gives individual MSPs, or groups of MSPs, the chance to represent their constituents' concerns, passing laws about issues that concern them. The first step in making a new law is to propose a Bill: a draft law.

TYPES OF BILLS

There are a number of different types of Bills, each given a different name depending on who introduced them. Some of these are given below.

Executive (Government) Bills

These are Bills introduced by the Cabinet secretary – government official – who is in charge of the policy area that the Bill falls under. For example, the Justice Secretary could introduce Bills to change the ways the police or courts operate.

Members' Bills

These are Bills introduced by an MSP who is not a member of the government. To introduce a Member's Bill to parliament, the proposal needs to be supported by 18 other MSPs from at least half of the parties in parliament. The Bill must also be different to any Bills the government plans to introduce.

Committee Bills

Conveners (leaders) of Scottish Parliament committees (see pages 20–21) can introduce Bills related to their committee's policy area. For example, the Education and Culture Committee can introduce a Bill about the way that schools operate.

Private Bills

Private Bills are Bills that give a person or organisation particular powers or benefits that are greater than the law would normally allow. These are dealt with in a different way to the Bills above, as are Hybrid Bills.

Hybrid Bills

Hybrid Bills are Bills that affect some more than others. They are usually to do with planning or development projects. The first one considered by the Scottish Parliament was to allow a new crossing for the River Forth.

DON'T FORGET

Introducing a Bill gives MSPs a chance to represent their constituents by highlighting an issue of particular concern to their constituents.

THE LEGISLATIVE PROCESS

There are a number of stages that a Bill must pass through before it can become a law. These occur in four main stages.

Stage 1

When a government or Member's Bill is proposed, the relevant committee will conduct an inquiry into the proposal. They will investigate possible effects of the Bills, including hearing evidence from expert witnesses. The committee will publish a report on what it finds (Committee Bills miss this stage out).

The parliament then has a short debate and vote on the general principles of the Bill. This just means that the MSPs think it is worth the parliament's time to consider. If MSPs don't agree to these principles, the Bill fails. If they agree, it passes on to the next stage.

contd

Stage 2

In stage 2, the relevant committee looks at the proposed Bill in great detail. This stage is called detailed consideration. The committee can make changes, or amendments, to the Bill at this stage.

Stage 3

The amended Bill is then passed to the whole Scottish Parliament for discussion. MSPs can make further amendments to the Bill at this stage. MSPs then vote on the Bill. If less than half (a minority) of MSPs vote in favour of the Bill, it fails. If more than half (a majority) vote in favour, it moves to the next stage.

Summary of Scottish Parliament Legislation, May 16 – June 18

Legislation	Government	Member's	Private	Committee	Total
Bills in progress	12	0	1	0	13
Bills awaiting Royal Assent	5	0	0	0	5
Acts of the Scottish Parliament	13	2	2	0	17
Total	30	2	3	0	35

(SPICe, 2018)

After stage 3

After the Scottish Parliament has voted in favour of a Bill, the Secretary of State for Scotland and a legal expert called the Advocate General for Scotland (both UK Government officials) have 4 weeks to decide if they object to the law because it interferes with the UK's national security or is not a decision the Scottish Parliament has the power to make. If they propose changes, the Bill must be reconsidered in the Scottish Parliament.

Usually there are no objections at this stage, and the Bill is passed to the monarch for Royal Assent, when the Queen officially signs the Bill into law.

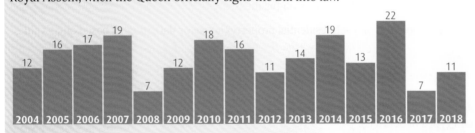

Acts of the Scottish Parliament 2004–2017.

So far, in 2018, there have been 11 bills which have passed through the full legislative process and became Acts of the Scottish Parliament. These include:

- Land and Buildings Transaction Tax (Relief from Additional Amount) (Scotland) Act 2018
- Civil Litigation (Expenses and Group Proceedings) (Scotland) Act 2018
- Social Security (Scotland) Act 2018

DON'T FORGET

Each and every Bill is proposed in order to make life in Scotland better, whoever introduces it.

ONLINE TEST

Test yourself on the legislative process in Scotland at www.brightredbooks.net/N5ModernStudies.

ONLINE

Head to the BrightRed Digital Zone for a great class activity on Passing a Private Members' Bill!

THINGS TO DO AND THINK ABOUT

1 Research and make notes on a Bill the Scottish Parliament is looking at just now using the Scottish Parliament's 'Current Bills' page: http://www.scottish.parliament.uk/parliamentarybusiness/Bills/576.aspx.

   a What type of Bill is it? Who introduced it?

   b What does it hope to achieve?

   c What stage is it at?

   d Present the Act to the class.

2 Do the same for a recent Act of the Scottish Parliament: http://www.scottish.parliament.uk/parliamentarybusiness/Bills/610.aspx.

LOCAL COUNCILS

THE PROVISION OF SERVICES

Local councils (or local authorities) are responsible for providing services in their local area, such as education, leisure and public transport.

There are 32 local authorities in Scotland, ranging in population from under 20,000 in Orkney to over 600,000 in Glasgow, and in size from 26 square miles in Dundee to 12,437 square miles in the Highlands.

Each local authority area is run by a council. Local residents elect councillors to represent them in the council, usually every 4 years. Local councillors are elected using the single transferable vote system (see pages 34–35). Three or four councillors are elected to represent a specific area, called a **ward**. The work of local councillors is discussed on pages 26–27.

FUNDING

Local councils get most (around 85%) of their money in a block grant from the Scottish Government. The rest of their money comes from:

- grants for **capital expenditure**: the Scottish Government often gives local authorities money for expensive projects, like new schools or bridges
- non-domestic rates: local taxes on businesses
- **council tax**: paid on each residential property (house or flat), roughly based on its value.

FACT

In total, there are 1227 local councillors in Scotland.

COUNCIL SERVICES

Each local authority is responsible for providing services in their area. There are three main types of services:

- mandatory services: these are services that the law says local councils have to provide, such as education and social work
- permissive services: councils do not have to provide these, but usually choose to, such as leisure centres
- discretionary services: councils may choose to give money to specific programmes.

Councils also have regulatory powers. This means awarding health and safety certificates to restaurants and take-aways, planning permission for building works, and licences to taxis, bars and nightclubs.

Selected local council services: Housing and planning, Economic development, Roads and transport, The environment, Education, Waste management – recycling and bins, Arts, culture and sport, Social work, Libraries, Leisure

ONLINE TEST

Take the test on local council services and funding at www.brightredbooks.net/N5ModernStudies.

Local councils make their own decisions and officially only have to answer to the people (and voters) in their area. However, there are examples of the Scottish Government influencing the decisions of local councils. Some of these are discussed in the case studies below.

CASE STUDIES

Edinburgh trams

Transport is a devolved issue, and is also an issue under local authority control. Back in 2002, Transport Initiatives Edinburgh ('Tie') concluded that congestion was going to be a significant challenge in the future, as Edinburgh's population was predicted to increase.

The initial tram network was predicted to cost £498m, and go from Newbridge and Edinburgh Airport down to Leith and Crewe Toll and be completed by summer 2011.

In June 2007, the Scottish Parliament voted to provide a maximum of £500m to City of Edinburgh Council for this capital expenditure project. However, as the project got underway a number of problems began to surface including contract disputes.

By 2011, plans for a wider tram network had been shelved and it was decided that the trams would be on one line, from the airport into the city. On 25 August 2011, City of Edinburgh Council held a vote on whether to stop the trams at Haymarket. The vote passed.

However, five days later, the then Finance Secretary (now Deputy First Minister) John Swinney said that the Scottish Government would not pay its final payment of £72m, as the plans had changed too much. This Scottish Government decision forced City of Edinburgh Council to have another vote, and on 2 September 2011, the vote passed 28/15 in favour of continuing to St Andrew Square.

Trump golf course

In 2006, long before becoming US President, billionaire Donald Trump announced plans to build a new golf centre, costing up to £1bn, with two courses, a hotel and a holiday home complex, on the Menie Estate in Aberdeenshire. The First Minister of the time, Jack (now Lord) McConnell, met Mr Trump twice at this stage. This caused concern amongst some, with a Green Party spokesperson saying: 'Mr McConnell is clearly backing this project but it's actually a job for the local council to decide and not him.'

Groups such as Scottish Natural Heritage, the Royal Society for the Protection of Birds (RSPB) and Sustainable Aberdeenshire also raised concerns about the damage that the course could do to the local scenery and bird populations.

However, in November 2008, the Scottish Government approved the golf resort.

Since granting the development there has been a number of disagreements between Trump, local residents and the Scottish Government including:

- Trump attempting to block the development of an offshore wind farm near his golf course in 2015. This led to numerous public disagreements with former First Minister, Alex Salmond, who said 'Donald Trump is a wonderful person until you disagree with him'. The wind farm was given the go-ahead and is now complete.

- Trump claimed his golf development in Aberdeenshire would create circa 6000 jobs, to date, only 150 are actually employed.

- Trump has been repeatedly accused of intimidating local residents by erecting fences, cutting off water and electricity supplies and threatening them with legal action.

- Trump was stripped of his honorary degree by Robert Gordon University in 2015.

DON'T FORGET

Capital expenditure is usually funded with a large Scottish Government grant.

FACT

In late 2017 following an independent inquiry, it was announced that final cost of the Edinburgh Tram Project would be in excess of £1 billion which includes the scheme cost as well as interest payments on borrowing over three decades.

FACT

When President Trump visited Scotland in July 2018, the trip reportedly cost the UK Government circa £5m

FACT

Trump has been accused of attempting to 'blackmail Scotland' by threatening to pull out his substantial investments.

THINGS TO DO AND THINK ABOUT

1 Make a list of all the ways you have used council services in the past week. How important is the local council to your daily life?

2 Write a summary (two or three paragraphs) of each of the case studies above. What do they tell us about the power that local councils have compared to those of the Scottish Government?

WORK OF LOCAL COUNCILLORS

THE COMPOSITION OF LOCAL COUNCILS

Local councils are made up of elected councillors. There are 1227 councillors in total in Scotland. Each **ward**, or area, elects three or four councillors. They are elected using the single transferable vote system (see pages 34–35).

Councillors earn a basic salary of £16,927 (from 4th May 2017), or more if they are an opposition spokesperson or are the convener of a committee (see below). Council leaders can earn up to £50,783 per year, depending on the size of their local authority.

Councillors have a number of main roles that they must fulfil in order to provide local solutions for local problems. Malcolm Bell, Convener of Shetland Islands Council (SIC), puts it like this:

'My personal belief is that decision making (and the ability to fund and be accountable for such decisions) should be devolved to the lowest possible level. There is a great deal of evidence that good decisions are made in this environment ... Local authorities need the freedom to provide local services according to the situation pertaining in their area. One size does not fit all.'

Convener Malcolm Bell.

Councillor Mandy Morgan.

SURGERIES

Councillors are elected by voters to represent their concerns and opinions when important local decisions are made. In order to learn about their constituents' concerns, councillors hold **surgeries**. These are open meetings where any resident can meet their councillor and raise any issues they feel strongly about or ask questions about what the council is doing. Mandy Morgan, councillor for the North East Ward in Glasgow, holds surgeries three times a month in different places around the city. Councillors can then represent their constituents by raising these concerns within the council or at a higher level.

FULL COUNCIL MEETINGS

Many important council decisions are taken by a meeting of the full council. These meetings occur when the entire council meets together to make decisions about what to do in their area. Decisions are made by voting. When voting, councillors don't just base their decisions on their own opinion, but also what their party wants and the views that they have heard from their constituents, for example at surgeries.

Meetings are held according to that council's rules. For example, the City of Edinburgh Council usually meets once a month. Full council meetings are open to the public so anyone can attend and watch decisions being made. The **agenda** and **minutes** (written record) of council meetings are made available to the public.

COMMITTEES

Local councillors may also join council committees. These are small groups of councillors who propose new decisions for the council or scrutinise (closely examine) decisions the council has already made. Each committee works on a different topic or policy area. For example, the City of Edinburgh Council has an Education, Children and Families Committee. Its convener (leader) is Councillor Ian Perry.

If a local resident has a complaint or wants to raise an issue about this topic area, they can contact a member of this committee even if they are not from that councillor's area.

DELIVERING SERVICES

As well as committees, councillors can also be involved in arm's-length external organisations (ALEOs). These are organisations outside the council that the council can use to deliver services like leisure services, property maintenance, transport or economic development. At this time of budget cuts, councils are beginning to use ALEOs more, as using them can often be cheaper than using the council's own departments.

Councillors may also be appointed to sit on a Joint Board. These boards are responsible for overseeing the delivery of council services. For example, councillors from City of Edinburgh, Fife, Perth and Kinross and West Lothian Councils sat on the Forth Estuary Transport Authority (FETA), which was responsible for the maintenance and operation of the Forth Road Bridge. FETA was disbanded in 2015, with responsibility for the Forth Road Bridge and the Queensferry crossing going to Amey PLC who won the contract.

Queensferry Crossing.

WORKING WITH OTHER REPRESENTATIVES

In order to make the best decisions possible, local councillors often meet with other representatives. Councillors might meet with community councillors, MSPs or MPs if they think this will help to resolve the issue. For example, if a constituent raised a concern about health care in their ward, their councillor could discuss the issue with the area's MSPs and ask them to raise it in the Scottish Parliament.

CELEBRATING LOCAL SUCCESSES

Local councillors are, of course, primarily concerned with very local issues. As well as providing services and fixing problems, councils are also very keen to celebrate achievements or efforts made by people in the local area.

Shetland Islands Council Convener Malcolm Bell presents Diamond Jubilee certificates and badges to Shetland's School Crossing Patrol Officers.

THINGS TO DO AND THINK ABOUT

1 Find out how your local councillor is using your council's webpage.

2 Try to find examples of your local councillors working in each of the ways described above.

   Use what you find to make an A4 poster called 'The work of local councillors'.

3 How important do you think local councils are in Scotland?

   Use what you have learned about the parliament and local councils to write a report explaining what you think.

 ONLINE TEST

Take the test on local councillors at www. brightredbooks.net/ N5ModernStudies.

ELECTIONS AND ELECTION CAMPAIGNS

REPRESENTATIVE DEMOCRACY

The UK is a **representative democracy**. This means that the people have power (democracy) and that they choose people to speak up for them when important decisions are made (representatives).

These representatives are voted in by their constituents in elections. This means that every few years, the public get a chance to choose who to send to council or parliament to make decisions for them. Before these election days, there is a set period of time in which the **candidates** and their parties can campaign to attempt to win votes: **election campaigns**.

WHY HAVE ELECTION CAMPAIGNS?

Election campaigns perform a number of functions in a democracy.

First, they tell the public about the candidates' policies. The **electorate** (voters) will have a choice of people to vote for in the election, so the parties and candidates spend a lot of time and effort telling the electorate what they stand for.

Second, election campaigns highlight local concerns to candidates. Election campaigns give the public a chance to speak face to face with candidates, who will learn a lot over this time about what the electorate see as the really important issues in their area. These may be very different from the policies or priorities of the candidate's party.

Third, election campaigns give candidates and parties in power the chance to highlight their achievements since the last election. Candidates want re-election (to be voted in again) and so will do everything they can to make sure that the electorate know about all of their achievements in the role.

Equally, election campaigns give opposing candidates and parties the chance to highlight the candidate's or party in power's failures since the last election. This is called **negative campaigning**.

During these periods, politics is given more coverage in the media, for example in **party election broadcasts** (see pages 40–41) and many people begin discussing politics more.

STANDING AS A CANDIDATE

Those who are particularly committed to making their local area a better place to live may choose to stand as a candidate in an election. People may stand as an independent candidate or for a party. Depending on the type of election, one or more candidate per party can stand for election in an area.

Standing as a candidate is a considerable time commitment. Candidates spend time **canvassing** the voters in their area. This means going door-to-door, introducing themselves to prospective voters, explaining policies and listening to the concerns of voters.

Candidates also appear in the media, attempting to show themselves and their policies in a good light. For example, a candidate for a local council election may write a letter to the local newspaper, while a candidate for a parliamentary seat may try to get on a regional TV news bulletin. The local area may hold a **hustings**, a public event where the candidates give speeches and are asked questions about themselves and their policies.

Canvassing voters

Personal qualities of candidates

Potential candidates are trying to appeal to voters to choose them over the other candidates. Voters are usually more likely to vote for candidates they

contd

see as trustworthy, honest, qualified for and capable of doing the job, and hardworking. Being a confident public speaker is also extremely useful. There are, however, a number of characteristics that seem to help people get elected. Successfully elected candidates (like MPs and MSPs) are much more likely than the electorate to be male, white, middle-aged, university graduates and reasonably wealthy.

PARTICIPATING IN ELECTION CAMPAIGNS

Without standing as a candidate, there are many ways that members of the public can participate in an election campaign.

Joining a political party

By joining a political party members of the public can share their point of view and help their party come up with policies that fit with many members' views. To join a party, a membership fee must be paid and the money that parties raise this way can contribute a great deal towards paying the costs of a campaign. Members (or non-members) can also donate to a campaign whenever they want. Members of parties can also accompany or assist their party/candidate when canvassing.

Non-party members

Without joining a party, the public can participate in election campaigns by publicising a supported party or candidate. This can be done through putting up posters in windows, handing out leaflets containing policies, or putting up signs in the garden or on lampposts. Of course, party members can also do this. Members of the public can attend hustings to learn more about the different candidates standing in their area. They can raise concerns that they have, knowing that the candidates will have to respond then and there.

People can also become more educated about the candidates and parties standing for election. Watching party election broadcasts (see pages 40–41) on TV or reading election leaflets and election coverage in the newspapers will mean that on election day the voter will be sure to make a reasoned decision. To help voters do this, each party publishes a manifesto, a document that contains all their policies.

WHY IS IT IMPORTANT TO VOTE?

Elections are the time, every few years, when the public gets to choose the people who will make the decisions that affect us all every day. Once elected, representatives have a **mandate** (power and right) to make these important decisions. It is therefore crucially important that the people voted into power reflect the opinions of the public.

Those who chose not to vote may not be happy with the decisions their representatives make, but they have lost their right to complain if they didn't help inform the electoral process by voting.

Voting is a democratic right. As with all rights, it comes with a responsibility: in this case to use it. It is not a right that everyone in Scotland has always had, and is one that many people around the world are still fighting and dying for, such as in the Arab Spring (see pages 102–103). Despite this, many people do not bother to vote in Scotland in the UK. This is called apathy. The **turnout** (percentage of people who could vote who actually do) is lower than you might think.

THINGS TO DO AND THINK ABOUT

1 Find at least three parties' manifestos online. Compare the policies each party has in a certain area, e.g. tax.
2 Watch some party election broadcasts on YouTube. What sort of pictures and words do they use to convince you to vote for them?
3 Imagine you are a candidate standing in an election. Prepare the introductory speech you would use when canvassing.

FACT

In 2018, selected UK political party membership is as follows:
Labour – 552,000
Conservative – 124,000
SNP – 118,200
Liberal Democrat – 101,500
Green – 41,073
UKIP – 21,200

FACT

Each of the main political parties has different membership fees depending on your circumstances (like if you're a student). The basic rates (2018) are:
Conservative £25.08
Labour £50.04
Liberal Democrat £12
(recommended £70)
SNP £12

FACT

Turnout in recent elections
UK general
election 2017 68.7%
Scottish Parliament
election 2016 55.6%
Scottish local council
elections 2017 46.9%

ONLINE TEST

Take the test on elections and election campaigns at www.brightredbooks.net/N5ModernStudies.

FIRST PAST THE POST

Isle of Wight: Constituency with largest electorate: 110,900.

Na h-Eileanan an Iar: Constituency with smallest electorate: 21,985.

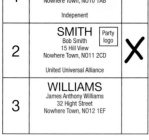

UK general election ballot paper.

THE IMPORTANCE OF CONSTITUENCIES

The **First Past The Post** (FPTP) voting system is used to elect MPs to the UK Parliament. For these elections, the UK is divided up into 650 constituencies (areas which elect a representative):

- 533 in England
- 40 in Wales
- 18 in Northern Ireland.
- 59 in Scotland

Constituency sizes and populations can be very different, but the average number of voters in each constituency (electorate) is approximately 66,250. Each constituency elects one MP.

UK parliamentary map

Boundary changes

Before the 2010 UK general election, both the Conservatives and the Liberal Democrats wanted to reduce the number of MPs. The Conservatives wanted 600, while the Liberal Democrats wanted 500 (elected under a different system). One reason for this is to save money: up to £12m a year. They also argued that it would make elections and politics fairer, as each person's vote would count a similar amount.

The coalition government introduced a Bill that proposed dividing the country up differently so that the number of voters in each constituency would be within 5% of 76,641 (exempt would be Na h-Eileanan an Iar, Orkney and Shetland, and the Isle of Wight).

Assuming the boundary changes are approved by MPs, they will come into effect in 2022. However, this change is not a forgone conclusion as it would lead to England having 32 fewer seats, Wales having 11 fewer seats, Scotland having 6 less seats and Northern Ireland having 1 less seat. Although this would bring cost savings, it would see a number of well-known politicians lose their jobs..

HOW TO VOTE

To vote in an FPTP election, voters get a sheet of paper with the names and parties of all the candidates written on it (a **ballot paper**). There is a maximum of one candidate per party in each constituency. Voters vote for a candidate by placing an 'X' in the box next to their preferred candidate's name.

In each seat, the candidate who gets the most votes (a **plurality** or simple majority) wins. This means that the winning candidate only needs to have one more vote than the candidate who comes second to win.

The closest result in the 2017 UK general election was in North East Fife, when Stephen Gethins of the SNP won with 13,743 votes which was just two more votes than Elizabeth Riches of the Liberal Democrats.

UK general election results 2017 (selected parties)

Party	Number of seats	Number of votes	Seats (%)	Votes (%)
Conservative	317	13,636,684	48.7	42.34
Labour	262	12,877,858	40.3	39.99
Liberal Democrat	12	2,371,861	1.84	7.37
Democratic Unionist Party (Northern Ireland)	10	292,316	1.53	0.91
SNP	35	977,568	5.38	3.4
Green	1	525,435	0.15	1.63

FACT ✓

Median parliamentary electorate	
England	72,400
Scotland	69,000
Northern Ireland	66,800
Wales	56,800

(Average constituency electorate across the UK.)

contd

FPTP has many advantages and disadvantages. Some of these are summarised below.

Advantages	Disadvantages
FPTP is the simplest voting system to understand for voters: it's how groups make most decisions.	As candidates only need to have a plurality to win, there are a large number of **wasted votes** (votes for a losing candidate) that count for nothing.
The voter is making a clear choice of which candidate they want to win the seat (or the party they want to form the government).	When a voter knows that there are only two candidates likely to win – and they don't support either of these – they may vote for their least-disliked candidate to stop their most-disliked from winning. This is called **tactical voting** and doesn't allow the voter to really express their choice or wishes.
Having one MP per constituency means that voters know who to contact with their problems and who is speaking up for them. This is called having a strong **constituency link**.	There are many seats where one party is incredibly likely to win: these are called **safe seats**. Other parties and candidates spend little time or money campaigning in safe seats, and instead campaign in seats they have a chance of winning, suggesting some votes count for more than others.
It is easy to count the votes and work out the winner: results are quickly found.	FPTP election results are usually very **disproportional** (the share of seats does not fairly represent the share of votes for a party). This often means that smaller parties do not get the number of seats they may deserve, and that votes for these parties are usually wasted votes.
FPTP normally leads to one of the two main parties winning most of the seats and forming a **majority government**. When this happens, they can carry out their policies reasonably quickly and easily.	FPTP doesn't always lead to a majority government. This leads to slower decision making and parties having to make compromises that nobody voted for.

THINGS TO DO AND THINK ABOUT

1   Use the 2017 UK general election results to find examples of the advantages and disadvantages of the first-past-the-post voting system.

2   Find out the name of your constituency and who your MP is using the UK Parliament website: http://findyourmp.parliament.uk/.

3   Find your constituency's result.

   a   Find out the share of votes your MP won with.

   b   Work out the number of wasted votes in your constituency.

4   Hold a class UK general election!

  • Each group will act as a constituency.

  • Each member of your group will be representing a candidate from a different political party: Conservative, Labour, Liberal Democrat, SNP, Green, etc.

  • Copy out the ballot paper, adding your group's name.

  • Vote for your preferred candidate by writing an 'X' in the box next to their name.

  • Copy and complete the table below using your class election results:

Party	Number of seats	Number of votes	Seats (%)	Votes (%)
Conservative				
Labour				
Liberal Democrat				
SNP				
Green				

What do your class results tell you about the first-past-the-post system?

VIDEO LINK

Check out 'BBC Class Clips – FPTP explained using pizza' at www.brightredbooks.net/N5ModernStudies

ONLINE TEST

Test your knowledge of FPTP online at www.brightredbooks.net/N5ModernStudies.

THE ADDITIONAL MEMBER SYSTEM

Election of the Scottish Parliament
You have **two** votes

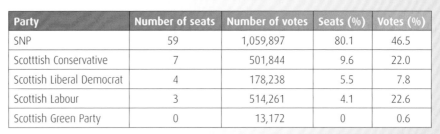

Scottish Parliament ballot paper.

CONSTITUENCIES AND REGIONS

The **Additional Member System** (AMS) is used to elect MSPs to the Scottish Parliament. For these elections, Scotland is divided up into 73 constituencies and 8 regions. Voters vote twice:

- once for a candidate in their constituency
- once for a party in their region.

Each of these votes is counted a different way to give more **proportional** results than FPTP. Because it mixes two types of voting system to do this, AMS is called a hybrid system.

AMS CONSTITUENCIES

Under AMS, each constituency elects one constituency MSP using FPTP. Each voter votes for a candidate by placing an 'X' next to the name of their chosen candidate. The candidate with the most votes (a **plurality**) wins. Seventy-three MSPs are elected this way.

Scottish Parliament elections 2016: constituencies scoreboard

Party	Number of seats	Number of votes	Seats (%)	Votes (%)
SNP	59	1,059,897	80.1	46.5
Scotttish Conservative	7	501,844	9.6	22.0
Scottish Liberal Democrat	4	178,238	5.5	7.8
Scottish Labour	3	514,261	4.1	22.6
Scottish Green Party	0	13,172	0	0.6

In 2016, the SNP had a disproportional number of constituency MSPs (a higher percentage of seats than their percentage of votes), while other parties had too few. This is where the additional (regional) members come into play.

Scottish Parliament
constituencies

AMS REGIONS

Under AMS, Scotland is also divided up into eight larger regions. Each region elects seven regional (list) MSPs.

To vote for regional MSPs, voters mark an 'X' next to their preferred party (not candidate). The parties – not voters – choose the order of the candidates on their list: the higher up the list a candidate is in their region, the more likely they are to get elected.

The regional votes for each party are used to top up the number of MSPs a party gets to give as proportional an overall result as possible. The regional list MSPs are the additional members the system is named after.

Scottish Parliament elections 2016: regional scoreboard

Party	Number of seats	Number of votes	Seats (%)	Votes (%)
Scotttish Conservative	24	524,222	42.9	22.9
Scottish Labour	21	435,919	37.5	19.1
Scottish Green Party	6	150,426	10.7	6.6
SNP	4	953,387	7.1	41.7
Scottish Liberal Democrat	1	119,284	1.8	5.2

Scottish Parliament regions.

DON'T FORGET

The regional votes for each party are used to top up the number of MSPs a party gets to give as proportional an overall result as possible.

contd

As you can see in the table, in 2016 the SNP were over-represented in constituency seats. To make the result more proportional, the SNP is under-represented in regional seats.

This is designed to give an overall result that is reasonably proportional.

Scottish Parliament elections 2016: overall result

Party	Constituency Seats	Regional Seats	Total Seats	+/- since 2011
Scottish National Party	59	4	63	-6
Scottish Conservatives	7	24	31	+16
Scottish Labour	3	21	24	-13
Scottish Green Party	0	6	6	+4
Scottish Liberal Democrats	4	1	5	-

VIDEO LINK

Watch 'BBC Class Clips – AMS explained' at www.brightredbooks.net/N5ModernStudies.

FACT

In 2016, the Scottish National Party lost their overall majority which they won in 2011.

ADVANTAGES AND DISADVANTAGES OF AMS

AMS has many advantages and disadvantages. Some of these are summarised below.

Advantages	Disadvantages
Voters have more choice as they can vote for a candidate they really like (even if they're not from the party they support) and also for their preferred party.	It could be confusing for some voters who may think one of the ballots is for a 'second choice'.
Small parties have a realistic chance of being elected.	Extremist parties could get elected.
Constituency MSPs keep a strong constituency link.	People may not even know who their regional MSP is, limiting their ability to really represent their constituents.
There are few wasted votes as the regional vote allows voters to have a say even if their constituency choice loses.	Regional MSPs may be seen as second-class MSPs – elected at the second attempt.
It gives roughly proportional results.	List MSPs are more accountable to the party leadership than to their voters, so voters may not be as well represented as the numbers suggest.
AMS is likely to lead to a coalition government, giving laws based on a variety of views: 2011 was the first time Scotland had a majority government under AMS.	Coalition governments can take a long time to reach decisions and/or make decisions that nobody voted for.

ONLINE TEST

Test your knowledge of AMS online at www.brightredbooks.net/N5ModernStudies.

THINGS TO DO AND THINK ABOUT

1 Use the 2016 Scottish Parliament election results to find examples of the advantages and disadvantages of the additional member system.

2 Find your constituency's result from the 2016 Scottish Parliament election.
   - Find out the share of votes your constituency MSP won with.
   - Work out the number of wasted votes in your constituency.

3 Find out your region's result from the 2016 Scottish Parliament election.
   - Find out which parties are represented in your region.

THE SINGLE TRANSFERABLE VOTE

HOW STV WORKS

The **Single Transferable Vote** (STV) system is used to elect local councillors in Scotland. Local elections in Scotland did use FPTP, but the Liberal Democrats bargained with Labour in the 2003–2007 coalition government to have STV introduced in time for the 2007 elections.

STV is a form of proportional representation. This means that the election results should mean that the share of representatives elected for each party should quite closely reflect the share of votes for that party.

Scotland is divided up into 32 local authorities, which are responsible for making local decisions in their area (see pages 24–25). Each of these local authorities is divided up into a number of multi-member wards (like mini-constituencies). Each ward elects three or four councillors. This means that more densely populated areas (cities) have more, and geographically smaller, wards. More rural areas (the countryside) have fewer, geographically larger, wards.

City of Edinburgh Council wards.

HOW TO VOTE

To vote in an STV election, voters are given a sheet of paper with the names of all the candidates on it (a ballot paper). Parties are able to put forward many candidates for each ward. This is because three or four councillors are elected for each ward, and of course each party wants to have as many elected as possible!

To vote, voters number the candidates in order of preference ('1' being the first choice, '2' being next favourite, and so on).

In order to be elected, a candidate does not need a majority of votes, just a **quota**, or share of votes. The quota required depends on the size of the electorate (number of voters) and the number of councillors to be elected in that ward. For a four-member ward, the quota is 20% of the total vote; for a three-member ward, the quota is 25% of the total vote.

In the Edinburgh ward of Meadows/Morningside, Nick Cook won 22.2% of the first preference ('1') votes and he was therefore elected at stage 1.

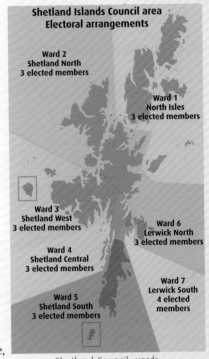

Shetland Council wards.

Local Government Election Results 2017

Ward 10 – Meadows/Morningside

Candidates Elected

Name	Party	Stage Elected
Nick Cook	Scottish Conservative and Unionist	One
Melanie Main	Scottish Green Party	Three
Neil Ross	Scottish Liberal Democrats	Five
Mandy Watt	Scottish Labour Party	Five

Results from City of Edinburgh Council, Meadows/Morningside ward, 2017.

contd

Once a candidate is elected (has met the quota), any votes they still have are called **surplus votes**. These votes are then reallocated (redistributed) to the next-preference candidates. For example, if the candidate voted '1' on a ballot already has more than the quota of votes, any surplus vote is reallocated to the candidate voted '2'. Each time votes are reallocated, this is called a stage of counting.

If there are still councillors to be elected after all the elected candidates' surplus votes have been redistributed, then the candidate with the fewest votes by that stage is eliminated, and their next-preference votes are reallocated to the other candidates.

This means that very few votes are wasted, as nearly all of them will contribute to the result at some stage.

	2012	2017	Percentage point change 2012–2017
Scottish Conservative & Unionist Party	115	276	140.0%
Scottish Labour Party	394	262	-33.5%
Scottish Liberal Democrats	71	67	-5.6%
Scottish National Party (SNP)	425	431	1.4%
Independents	200	168	-16.0%
Scottish Green Party	14	19	35.7%
Others	4	4	0.0%
Total	1223	1227	0.3%

STV has many advantages and disadvantages. Some of these are summarised below.

Advantages	Disadvantages
STV results in fewer wasted votes. There is no need for tactical voting, and voters may be more encouraged to vote when they can see that their vote counts.	Counting the votes takes a long time and many stages. It may take some time for people to know who is representing them.
STV gives voters more choice than any other voting system. Voters can choose not just a candidate from one party, but can rank-order all the candidates, from every party.	Voters may not know any candidates, never mind many from one party. In this case, it may be better to have parties put forward their best candidates for their safest seats.
As there are multi-member wards, parties are likely to try to appeal to as many voters as they can. This means they might put forward more female and ethnic minority candidates.	In large multi-member wards, with many candidates from the same party, the **ballot paper** may be big and confusing.
After the election, constituents have a choice of councillors to approach with their concerns.	To have enough voters, some wards are extremely large. Voters in remote areas of such wards may rarely see any councillors.
STV is likely to lead to a coalition local government or one under no overall control, giving laws based on a variety of views.	Coalition governments can take a long time to reach decisions and/or make decisions that nobody voted for.

VIDEO LINK

Check out 'BBC Class Clips – STV explained using ceilidh dancers' at www.brightredbooks.net/ N5ModernStudies.

ONLINE TEST

Test your knowledge of STV online at www. brightredbooks.net/ N5ModernStudies.

THINGS TO DO AND THINK ABOUT

1 Find out which local authority you live in and use their website to find out the results of the 2017 local elections in your ward.

Which stage was each councillor elected in?

2 What examples can you find of the advantages and disadvantages of STV using 2017 local council elections:
- in your ward
- in your council
- across the whole of Scotland?

3 Hold a class STV election!
- Get yourselves into groups of three or four people.
- Each group will represent a different political party: Conservative, Independent, Labour, Liberal Democrat, local issue party (make some up!), SNP, etc.
- Copy out the ballot paper, adding the names of all the candidates.
- Vote by numbering your candidates in order of preference: '1' being the highest, '2' next and so on.
- Work out the election results.

a What do your class results tell you about STV?

b How many votes were wasted?

PRESSURE GROUPS

DON'T FORGET

Pressure groups allow people to participate directly in politics

WHY JOIN A PRESSURE GROUP?

Pressure groups are organisations of people who all believe strongly in the same cause or issue. They aim to influence governments or other decision makers. By working together, pressure groups are likely to be more successful than individual people working alone: strength in numbers.

Elections are years apart, so joining a pressure group gives the public a more regular chance to let those in power know what they think. Pressure group action can also be a much more clear and powerful statement than voting.

Many of the public are disillusioned with political parties, politicians and elections. Pressure groups give the public a different way of getting involved in politics.

Insider pressure groups

Confederation of British Industry

National Farmers Union (Scotland)

British Medical Association (Scotland)

Outsider pressure groups

Animal Liberation Front

TYPES OF PRESSURE GROUPS

There are two main types of pressure groups in Scotland and the UK. Insider pressure groups are pressure groups that work closely and formally with the government and political parties. They are usually experts in a particular area of important government policy, and so the government benefits from this group's knowledge and skills in the area. The British Medical Association (BMA) and BMA Scotland (which also act as trade unions) hold meetings with government ministers and their departments, and provide the relevant parliament with research evidence for debates and expert witnesses for committee inquiries.

Outsider pressure groups are pressure groups that do not have such privileged access to decision makers. Unlike insider pressure groups, they cannot rely on being able to have face-to-face time to persuade the government about their point of view. This makes it more difficult to influence policy, so outsider pressure groups often have to resort to more extreme measures to get their point across.

PRESSURE GROUP ACTION

There are many different types of action that pressure groups can take when they are concerned about an issue. Some of these are legal and official, others are not.

Lobbying

Pressure groups have the right to try to meet MPs and MSPs to try to convince them about the issue they are concerned with. This can be done through letter, or by actually going to parliament to try to meet the MP or MSP face to face.

Petitions

Pressure groups often use petitions to put their point across. **Petitions** are calls for action by decision makers, which the public can sign if they agree with the action they want to happen. The more people who sign them, the more likely the decision maker is to consider taking that action. These days, petitions are usually done online: e-petitions.

The Scottish Parliament Public Petitions Committee exists only to consider petitions that are submitted by concerned groups (or even individuals). They even provide a template, an online petition tool, to make it easy for people to have a say.

If an e-petition to the UK Government gets 100,000 signatures, it will be debated by the House of Commons. An MP can, however, choose to represent the views expressed in a petition by personally raising the issue in parliament.

contd

International pressure group Greenpeace presented a 120,097-signature petition to the Environment Secretary Michael Gove and Chancellor Philip Hammond asking them to 'Please keep your promise – give us a watchdog that works!' Greenpeace are concerned that post-Brexit, environmental standards will be compromised and a 'green Brexit' will not be delivered.

Demonstrations and protests

Demonstrations and protests allow pressure groups to gain a lot of media attention for their cause. Gaining media attention allows the general public to hear about the pressure group's cause, and also allows the government and other decision makers to see how strongly people feel about the issue. Protesting is legal, but occasionally things get out of hand and some people are arrested.

On 14th April 2018, pro-European pressure groups including Open Britain and Britain for Europe participated in over 350 demonstrations across the length and breadth of the UK calling for another Brexit referendum.

Direct action

When a pressure group feels that it has exhausted all other ways of effecting change, they may resort to direct action. This is where a pressure group takes the law into their own hands and changes what they feel strongly about themselves. This form of pressure group action is illegal and its members (and perhaps even leadership) can be arrested because of it.

On 16 July 2012, Greenpeace activists shut down 74 Shell petrol stations in London and Edinburgh in protest at the company's plans to drill for oil in the Arctic. There were 24 arrests: 18 in London and 6 in Edinburgh.

A much more extreme example is the frequent actions of the Animal Liberation Front. This pressure group campaigns for the freedom of animals from ownership by companies. It takes extreme and highly illegal action to reach its aims, calling for 'abolition by any means necessary'.

Pressure groups and the media

Pressure groups aim to get the public interested in an issue, and get the government to do something about it. Getting the media's attention is a key way they can do this.

First, pressure groups hope that by raising the profile of their chosen issue, they can get many more members to join the group. This will give them more resources (active members and money) to further build their campaign. They will have increased strength in numbers. If getting a campaign shown in the media convinces the public, the government and other political parties might start to support it in the hope of attracting votes at the next election.

Large campaigns may force the companies or organisations directly involved to change the way they operate, without the need for government action, in order to look good to their customers. When UK Uncut (and others) highlighted Starbucks' limited tax payments, the company volunteered to pay £20m to the government. UK Uncut described it as 'a desperate attempt to deflect public pressure'.

VIDEO LINK

In the aftermath of the Grenfell Tower tragedy, hundreds of protesters took to the streets of London to vent their frustration at the way in which the UK Government dealt with the incident. Watch at www.brighredbooks.net/N5ModernStudies.

VIDEO LINK

Watch the 'Animal Liberation Front video' at www.brightredbooks.net/N5ModernStudies.

Rights	Responsibilities
To recruit new members and speak on their behalf	To truly represent the views of their members
To give out or publish information flyers and posters highlighting their cause	To ensure that all information is true and that nobody has their reputation damaged through untrue accusations
To criticise the government or other decision makers	
To protest and demonstrate	To inform police beforehand, allowing police to minimise disruption to the public by re-routing traffic, for example
	To remain within the law

Rights and responsibilities of pressure groups

THINGS TO DO AND THINK ABOUT

1 Find other examples of each of the types of pressure group action listed above. You can use an internet search like 'pressure group protest 2018' to get you started.

2 Research and make notes on a campaign by any of the pressure groups shown above.
   a What is the campaign about?
   b What does it hope to change?
   c What actions has it taken?

3 'The anti-cuts demonstrations of 26 March 2012 showed the best and the worst sides of pressure group action'. (View of a journalist).
   Watch the video at http://www.guardian.com/society/2011/mar/27/anti-cuts-protest-police-arrest-200 and give evidence to support this point of view.

ONLINE TEST

Take the test on pressure groups online at www.brightredbooks.net/N5ModernStudies.

TRADE UNIONS

WHY JOIN A TRADE UNION?

Trade unions are organisations that exist to represent workers or employees. Most employers want to cut down on costs by having workers work longer and paying as low wages as possible, while most employees would prefer more time off and higher pay for the work they do. Trade unions give workers strength in numbers in their discussions with their employers. Each workplace will have a union representative whom members can meet with if they need assistance and who will communicate with the union on their behalf. A union representative is also called a **shop steward**.

AIMS OF TRADE UNIONS

Trade unions have a number of main aims. First, they seek to represent their workers when they are unhappy at work. Second, they educate members about their rights in the workplace. They also negotiate on members' behalf when working conditions like pay are to change, providing strength in numbers.

TYPES OF TRADE UNION

There are three main types of trade union in the UK. Craft unions represent workers with a particular skill. There are very few of these in the UK now, but one example is Equity, which represents actors and models.

Industrial unions represent all workers in one industry who have different skills. An example of this is ASLEF, the Association of Locomotive Engineers and Firemen.

General unions represent workers from different industries. Unite is a general union and is the UK's biggest union.

TRADE UNION ACTION

There are many ways trade unions can take action in order to fulfil their aims.

Advice

Shop stewards (union representatives) can tell the union's members about how they can and should act in any work-based situation. On a wider scale, trade unions also often publish documents, widely available online, which detail the rights workers have in certain circumstances.

Negotiation

Trade unions can represent their members within the workplace during individual disputes, usually through the shop steward having meetings with the management. If a worker feels they are being unfairly pressured to do overtime, their shop steward could discuss this with management. When many workers are to be affected by bigger changes in an industry, trade unions will try to meet with those making the decisions in order to make the outcome as beneficial to its members as possible.

When there is to be a change in Scottish teachers' pay or conditions, the Educational Institute of Scotland (EIS) sends representatives to the Scottish Negotiating Committee for Teachers (SNCT) so that teachers are represented in discussions with local councils (employers) and the Scottish Government.

contd

Lobbying

Unison and the Trade Union Congress (TUC) ran a 'Pay Up Now' campaign in 2017 to bring an end to the pay cap for public sector workers. Public sector pay rose by just 4.4% between 2010–2016, when the cost of living for the same period rose by 22%. On the 17th October 2017, both unions held a joint-lobby of parliament to ensure their voices were heard.

Demonstrations

Trade unions often hold **demonstrations**, where members can meet and march together to highlight concerns the unions have. These demonstrations attract a great deal of media attention and draw the wider public's attention to the issues that the unions are raising.

Unite is running a 'Stop Universal Credit' campaign as they believe it is damaging society. On Thursday 24th May 2018, Unite members attended a Stop Universal Credit Day of Action to highlight the problems they believe are escalating as a result of Universal Credit being implemented. These problems included increased debt, rent-arrears leading to eviction and the explosion of food banks throughout the UK.

Industrial action

If negotiation fails, trade unions can take **industrial action**. This is any action that the trade union takes to disrupt normal working patterns. It is used as a last resort to show employers how seriously workers feel about the issue. Before starting industrial action, trade unions must hold a secret ballot of their members and the majority must approve it. There are many different forms of industrial action, some of which are detailed here.

An overtime ban is when workers refuse to work any time outside their contracted hours. This may stop the employer making as much profit as they would hope.

A work-to-rule is when a union tells it members to do exactly what their contracts tell them they have to and not anything more.

A strike is when workers refuse to work. This is the most well-known and strongest form of industrial action. This is the very last resort that unions can take. In May 2018, rail workers belonging to the union of Rail, Maritime and Transport workers (RMT) held a series of one-day strikes over a perceived change to the role of a train guard. This caused significant disruption to the train network and consequently public frustration.

Trade unions and the media

Trade unions seek to gain a great deal of media attention for their dispute. By informing the wider public through media coverage, they hope to gain wider public support. This in turn can, they hope, put pressure on their employers over the issue.

VIDEO LINK

Watch former Dynasty star, Stephanie Beacham, show her support for the 'Pay up Now' campaign at www.brightredbooks.net/N5ModernStudies.

ONLINE

To find out 10 reasons why Unite believe Universal Credit must be abolished, please visit www.brightredbooks.net/N5ModernStudies.

VIDEO LINK

Watch this short clip to find out more about the RMT strikes in 2018 www.brightredbooks.net/N5ModernStudies

ONLINE TEST

Take the test on trade unions online at www.brightredbooks.net/N5ModernStudies.

Rights of trade unions	Responsibilities of trade unions
To be consulted in and informed of decisions taken by the employer during a dispute.	To make sure that the shop steward is elected or chosen by the union members, and that the shop steward represents the members' true interests.
To have a shop steward (representative) in a place of work.	To represent the true interests of their members during any dispute.
To lobby local and national politicians or decision makers to try to gain their support for their cause, perhaps putting pressure on the employer about the issue.	To present the decision makers with the facts of the issue so they are fully informed before deciding whether or not to support the trade union over the issue.
To hold demonstrations to highlight their cause to the media and the public.	To not break the law during demonstrations.
	To inform police before a demonstration to allow them to plan for disruption.
To take part in industrial action: strikes, overtime bans, work-to-rules.	To hold a secret ballot of members before any industrial action is taken.
	To not force members to take part in any action.

THINGS TO DO AND THINK ABOUT

Research another trade union, perhaps the one that would represent you in your planned career: Find examples of this trade union representing their members in a range of ways.

THE MEDIA: TV

ROLE OF THE MEDIA

The **media** is crucial to how a democratic society works. A free press gives people the chance to learn about the decisions made by governments and parliaments. Representatives are chosen to speak up for the public; it is crucially important that the public have a chance to question them on their decisions and actions.

There are three main functions of the media in a democracy:

- to keep the public informed about what is going on
- to allow representatives' decisions to be scrutinised (looked at closely)
- to give the public a chance to express their points of view.

INFLUENCING DECISION MAKERS

In performing these roles, the media can have an important influence on the decisions made by those in power. Nearly everyone in Scotland and the UK sees or hears at least one form of media, so the message that the public receive from the media can have a big effect on the actions and popularity of the government and other parties and politicians.

FACT

TV licence costs 1 May 2018:
- £150.50 (colour TV)
- £50.50 (black and white TV)
- Free for those over-75 years old

TV

In the UK, TV coverage of political issues and parties must be neutral by law. This means that TV companies should allow parties a fair chance to put their point of views across and cannot show that they prefer one party over another. The BBC in particular is under strict control as the public pay for it through a licence fee.

Each of the TV stations in the UK devotes a considerable amount of time to political issues. The four terrestrial broadcasters (BBC, ITV/STV, Channel 4 and Channel 5) all have news bulletins as well as other current affairs or political shows such as Newsnight, Daily Politics, Dispatches, Question Time and Scotland Tonight.

In each of these programmes, however, the journalists and presenters are entitled to ask difficult and probing questions that can often make life very difficult for the politician in question even if she has the top job!

In May 2017, Prime Minister Theresa May was questioned very thoroughly by BBC presenter and journalist Andrew Neil on his show 'The Andrew Neil Interviews'.

Theresa May.

contd

Party political broadcasts and party election broadcasts

Party political broadcasts (PPBs) are TV (or radio) broadcasts produced by political parties in which they put forward their point of view or criticise opposition parties. Party election broadcasts (PEBs) are broadcasts of this type that are broadcast during an election campaign. They are one of very few ways that political parties can publicise their message through the media without any journalists or editors altering or interpreting it.

TV leaders' debates

Televised leaders' debates were held for the first time in the UK for the 2010 UK general election and the 2011 Scottish Parliamentary election. The three general election debates were on ITV, Sky TV and BBC, and attracted audiences of over 9 million, around 4 million and over 8 million viewers, respectively.

In the run up to the 2016 Scottish Parliament elections, three TV debates were held, two broadcast by the BBC (24th Match, 1st May) and one broadcast by STV (29th March). The politicians were asked a number of questions including:

- In what ways will the panellists use tax raising powers to improve the lives of Scottish people?

- When push comes to shove do you support fracking or not?

- What specific plans do you have to create more jobs?

- How are you going to protect the health budget with ever growing austerity?

VIDEO LINK

Watch the 2017 party election broadcasts for the Conservatives, Labour, Liberal Democrats and Greens, and the 2016 broadcast for the SNP at www.brightredbooks.net/N5ModernStudies.

FACT

During the final BBC debate, the #leadersdebate generated over 20,000 tweets highlighting the increased way in which society use social media to engage in politics.

Jeremy Corbyn (Labour), Theresa May (Conservative), and Tim Farron (Liberal Democrat).

Patrick Harvie (Greens), Kezia Dugdale (Labour), Nicola Sturgeon (SNP), Ruth Davidson (Conservative) and Willie Rennie (Liberal Democrat).

THINGS TO DO AND THINK ABOUT

Find TV or online coverage of a pressure group or trade union campaign. Does the coverage seem to be in favour of the action or not? Note down any parts of the report that make you think this.

ONLINE TEST

Take the 'Media' test online at www.brightredbooks.net/N5ModernStudies

THE MEDIA: NEWSPAPERS AND NEW MEDIA

NEWSPAPERS

Many people in Britain read a newspaper every day.

Unlike the broadcast media, TV and radio, newspapers are allowed to openly support a party. Owners and editors of newspapers hope that the way they present the parties, candidates and policies will influence the public into voting for a preferred candidate/party.

Newspaper ownership

According to a 2015 report from the Media Reform Coalition ownership of UK media is highly concentrated. The report, 'Who owns the UK Media?' highlights that News UK (*The Sun*), DMGT (the *Daily Mail*) and Trinity Mirror (the *Daily Mirror*) control over 70% of the national newspaper market. The Media Reform Coalition asserts that this poses a significant threat to news plurality choice.

Some people argue that with so many media outlets being owned by so few people or groups, fewer and fewer different political opinions will be heard. If an important role of the media is to inform the public, this could be damaging.

Newspapers and election campaigns

In the run-up to elections, newspapers often dedicate a considerable amount of space to their preferred party or candidate.

In the UK in 2010, *The Sun* supported the Conservative Party, 13 years after changing from the Conservatives to Labour.

Before the 2011 Scottish Election, *The Scottish Sun* performed a similar U-turn, supporting the SNP running the headline: 'Play it again, Salm', after warning voters in 2007 that 'vote SNP today and you put Scotland's head in a noose'.

Some people argue that newspapers influence the voters that read them and therefore have a large influence on the outcomes of elections. Others argue that the biggest newspapers switch to whichever party is likely to win, to seem in line with public opinion. Others argue that people will buy whichever newspaper backs up their opinion and so they don't affect the results of elections.

Newspapers and political coverage

Another way that the (non-broadcast) media can influence the government is through their coverage of government decisions. While the radio and TV have to be neutral about government actions – or at least treat each party in the same way – the print media can clearly show its displeasure at government decisions. By reporting the actions of government in a positive or negative light, the media hope the government will reconsider the decisions they don't like.

In these examples, Scotland's biggest two broadsheet newspapers disagreed about whether an independent Scotland could keep its banknotes: an important question for Finance Secretary John Swinney to answer.

contd

The Scotsman:
Coverage of Scottish bank notes question, 22 April 2013.

news.scotsman.com

Scottish independence: Banknotes safe - Swinney

The Herald:

Scottish banknotes at risk under Yes vote, warns Treasury

Monday 22 April 2013

NEW MEDIA

In previous elections people relied on the traditional media of TV, radio and newspapers. In recent elections, however, new digital media has begun to have an effect.

All parties now have Facebook groups, and nearly every MP and MSP has a Twitter account. This allows these parties and representatives to reach out to the public and journalists instantly. The public and journalists can also contact them in return.

Nearly all parties now have YouTube channels as well. This gives them a chance to broadcast their political messages over the internet to an almost infinite audience.

Mumsnet is a forum-based website where parents can speak about the issues that are important to them. Parents are, of course, a large proportion of the UK population, and it would help a politician get elected if they could win support from this group. In 2016, Labour leader Jeremy Corbyn held a live chat with members, following in the footsteps of previous high-profile politicians, and chatted about matters such as immigration, prostitution and post-Brexit Britain.

Rights and responsibilities of the media

Right	Responsibility
To report on what is happening in the country	To tell the truth
To investigate potential wrongdoing by public figures	To remain within the law and respect people's right to privacy (for example not to hack into people's phones)
To publish details of government spending	To not harm national security by revealing official secrets

THINGS TO DO AND THINK ABOUT

1   The media is a crucial factor in electoral success. Use examples on the past four pages to give arguments for and against this statement.

2   Try to find three different newspapers' coverage of the same political issue.

    Compare the ways these are covered. Are they in favour or against? How can you tell?

3   Have a look at the Facebook page or Twitter feed of one of the main political parties.

    What sort of comments and tweets do they post?

FACT

According to the Electoral Commission, political parties spent approximately £3.2m on Facebook advertising in 2017. It is the Conservative Party that spends the most on digital politics

SOURCE-BASED QUESTIONS: SELECTIVE IN THE USE OF FACTS

SELECTIVE IN THE USE OF FACTS

In source-based questions you are given a quote/view and have to describe ways in which the evidence supports the quote (shows it may be true) *and* ways in which the evidence does not support the quote (shows it may be untrue).

If you only discuss evidence on one side (supporting or opposing the quote), you will not be able to get full marks.

Each reason you give can get up to 3 marks, depending on how accurately you use your sources and how well you develop your argument.

Source 1: Selected female political representation in the UK 2000–2013

	2000	2004	2008	2013	Net change 2000/2013
Members of Parliament (MPs)	18.4%	18.1%	19.3%	22.5%	+4.1%
The Cabinet	21.7%	27.3%	26.1%	17.4%	−3.5%
Members of the Scottish Parliament (MSPs)	37.2%	39.5%	34.1%	35.7%	−1.5%
Local councillors	29.0%	30.0%	30.0%	32.0%	+3.0%
UK Members of the European Parliament (MEPs)	23.9%	24.4%	25.6%	33.3%	+9.4%

From *Sex and Power Report 2013*

Source 2: Women in politics

The late Baroness Thatcher was a very important and famous figure in British politics. She was elected as an MP in 1959 and became Conservative Party leader in 1975. She served as Britain's first and so far only female Prime Minister for 11 years from 1979 to 1990, winning three general election victories. She entered the House of Lords in 1992, and served until her death in April 2013.

Diane Abbott MP was elected to the UK Parliament in 1987, the first black woman to gain this position. She was appointed Shadow Minister for Public Health in 2010. Prime Minister David Cameron has pledged to make a third of his Cabinet female by 2015.

In the Labour Party leadership contest of 2010, Diane Abbott was the only woman to run, and she finished last in the ballot. The Green Party is currently the only UK party led by a woman.

In the Scottish Parliament, three out of the five parties are led by men. Johann Lamont is the leader of the Scottish Labour Party. First elected in 1999, and in every Scottish Parliament election since, she was elected leader in December 2011. Ruth Davidson MSP is leader of the Scottish Conservatives. She was elected to the Scottish Parliament in May 2011 and became leader in November of the same year.

The UK is currently ranked joint 58th in the world for female representation in a national parliament. The world leader is Rwanda, with 56%. At the current rate of progress, it will take 200 years – another 40 elections – to achieve an equal number of women in parliament in the UK.

Four of the last five leaders of the House of Lords have been women, and 41% of appointments made by the House of Lords Appointments Commission since 2004 have been women.

In the 2012 Scottish local council elections, one in four candidates was a woman. In one in seven council elections, there were only male candidates standing for election.

Source 3: Women as a percentage of MPs for each political party in 2000 and 2012

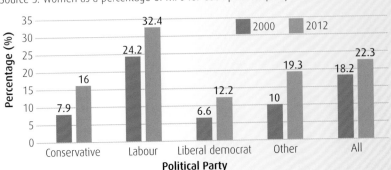

contd

Source 4: Claims of sexism in UK politics

In April 2011, David Cameron drew criticism for telling a female MP to 'calm down dear' during a Commons debate.

Former Conservative MP Louise Mensch demanded an apology from Labour MP Austin Mitchell in October 2012 after he tweeted to tell her 'a good wife doesn't disagree with her master in public', after her husband seemed to suggest a different reason for her leaving parliament.

Similarly, in January 2013, Murdo Fraser, MSP for Mid-Scotland and Fife, found out that the wife of former Liberal leader Lord Steel had said she was in favour of Scottish independence. He tweeted: 'Why is Lady Steel (apparently) pro-independence? Is he not master in his own house?'

In March 2013, Liberal Democrat youth leader Kav Kaushik said she may leave, and tweeted 'the sexism is too much for me now'.

In a speech in May 2013, Diane Abbott MP said that some parts of British culture see sexism and homophobia as normal, and expressed concern at the impression this was having on young men in the UK.

Answering a 'Selective in the use of facts' question

Using Sources 1, 2, 3 and 4 above explain why the view of Kevin Coutts is selective in the use of the facts.

> 'The UK political system is moving towards gender equality.'
>
> View of Kevin Coutts

In your answer you must:

- give evidence from the sources that supports Kevin Coutts's view; and

- give evidence from the sources that oppose Kevin Coutts's view.

    Your answer must be based on all four sources.   **10 marks**

A 3-mark section of an answer to this question could look like this:

Information to oppose the view	*There is information to oppose the view of Kevin Coutts where he states 'The UK political system is moving towards gender equality'*
Evaluative terminology	as the proportion of women in positions of power is *clearly decreasing* in many cases. *The share of women in the UK Cabinet*
Evidence from the sources which proves the exaggeration	*decreased from 21.7% to 17.4% between 2000 and 2013;* a significant 3.5% net *decrease (Source 1). Although* David Cameron has pledged to increase this number
The sources of the information	*to a third before the 2015 general election (Source 2),* he has already been accused *of sexism* in a parliamentary debate, *telling a female Labour MP to 'calm down dear'*
Developed discussion of the evidence	*(Source 4),* so it may be *very unlikely* that he will stick to this policy of treating women fairly.

To get full marks, this answer would need to have three or more sections:

- at least one other section that opposes his point of view

- at least one section using evidence that supports his point of view.

When arguing source-based questions, using fewer sections that use more sources and describe the argument in more detail may earn you more marks than a number of short sections with little of the evidence.

THINGS TO DO AND THINK ABOUT

Complete the 'selective in the use of facts' question above to get the rest of the 10 marks.

WHAT IS POVERTY?

People who live in **poverty** are considered to be those who struggle to pay for things they need. In the UK official poverty levels are measured by the Department of Work and Pensions using their Households Below the Average Income (HBAI) annual report, the latest figures for which were released in March 2018.

ABSOLUTE POVERTY

Globally, this term refers to those in less developed countries who may live on less than $1.90 per day and are deprived of basic human needs such as food, water, sanitation, health, shelter, education and access to support. In the UK absolute poverty is defined as anyone living on less than half the average UK annual income. In 2017 the average annual UK household income was measured at £27,271, so the absolute poverty level is £13,636.

The **United Nations** (UN) defines absolute poverty as 'a condition characterised by severe deprivation of basic human needs'.

RELATIVE POVERTY

Relative poverty is socially defined according to the society in which people live, e.g. those that are worse off than the majority of others where they are. A minimum standard, known as a poverty line, is set and anyone living below that amount is considered to be living in poverty. The poverty line is usually set at 60% of the median income (middle income in a range of all UK incomes).

ONLINE

Learn more by clicking the PSE link at www.brightredbooks.net/N5ModernStudies.

SOCIAL EXCLUSION

Social exclusion refers to those in poverty who are disconnected and are unable to participate in 'normal' society. People who are socially excluded cannot purchase goods or services that the average person would be able to buy, which has a severe impact on their quality of life.

GROUPS AT RISK OF POVERTY AND SOCIAL EXCLUSION

There are certain groups in society that are more at risk of poverty and social exclusion than others. The reasons for this are discussed later in this chapter.

Children and young people

Children are considered dependants, meaning that they cannot generate their own income and are reliant on adults such as their parents. Unfortunately, many children find themselves born into households in poverty and suffer as a consequence. Young people find it increasingly difficult to generate their own income, especially if they leave school at a young age with few academic qualifications.

- 34% of children in Glasgow were deemed to be living in poverty in 2017 (*The Child Poverty Map of the UK*, 2018, End Child Poverty).

- There were 34,000 Scottish youths unemployed in the period between November 2017 – January 2018 according to Scottish Government Labour Market Information (*The Herald, 1st April 2018*).

- Research from the TUC estimates that 3.1m children in the UK with working parents will be below the official breadline in 2018 (*The Guardian, 7th May 2018*).

contd

Working age adults

Working age adults are those people who are between age 16 and their retirement age. The age people can retire varies depending on when they were born.

This group may find themselves living in poverty due to unemployment or low pay:

- The number of people working part-time in Scotland and who wanted a full-time job rose from 70,000 in 2008 to 120,000 in 2012.
- As of March 2018 the UK unemployment percentage for working age adults was 4.2
- Although UK unemployment is currently at its lowest level in decades, underemployment is now higher in 2018 than it was during the 2008 Global crash (*Business Insider, 24th April 2018*).

The elderly

Most people decide to stop working and retire when they reach a certain age. The UK Government currently provides a **state pension** for many of those elderly people. The current maximum amount paid to any one person is £125.95 per week (plus £40 average top up) or £164.35 (for those reaching pension age after 2016). These payments increase slightly every year with rises in the cost of living. Working age adults are encouraged to take out supplementary private or **occupational pensions** throughout their working lives to top this state amount up when they retire. For some that extra saving is limited or impossible. This means there are many elderly people who are totally reliant on the state pension as their sole income when they retire and may find themselves struggling to pay for necessities and bills.

- According to 'UK Poverty 2017', a report compiled by the Joseph Rowntree Foundation, 1.9m pensioners 'do not have enough money to have an acceptable standard of living'.
- Women, those aged 80 to 84, those living alone, and Pakistani and Bangladeshi people are at greater risk of pensioner poverty than other social groups.

Summary table: the number of people living in UK households with below 60% of the average UK contemporary income (after housing costs are deducted):

	2016–2017 (millions)	2006–2007	Percentage change from 2006–2007 to 2016–2017
Children	30.3	30.5	−0.2
Working age adults	25.5	24.8	+0.7
Pensioners	15.8	18.7	−2.9

(Source: *JRF, 2017*)

THINGS TO DO AND THINK ABOUT

1 The UK Government spends time and money gathering information on current poverty levels. Give at least two reasons why the UK Government needs this information.

2 Why can the majority of people living in poverty in the UK be described as living in relative, and not absolute, poverty?

3 According to the Office for National Statistics the average household spent £554.20 per week in 2017 (after housing costs). A family in poverty has approximately 60% of that total amount to spend per week, reducing it to £332.52.
   - Working with a partner, use the figures above to decide where a family in poverty could reduce their spending to be within their budget but still have what their family needs.

4 The age people can receive their state pension in the UK varies depending on when they were born, e.g. if they were born in 1956 they may receive a state pension in 2022 when they are 66, but if they were born in 1979, they are not due to receive their state pension until age 68. Why do you think this is?

5 Answer this question using JRF statistics in the table above.
   'UK Government is successfully tackling poverty among all groups in society.'
   - Give reasons to support and oppose this statement.

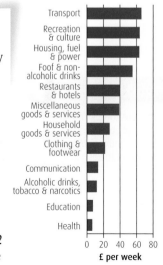

CAUSES OF POVERTY

The UK is the world's fifth-largest economy, yet over one fifth of the UK population live below its official **poverty line**, meaning that they experience life as a daily struggle.

There are many reasons for this and some groups of people are more likely to live in poverty than others.

UNEMPLOYMENT/WORKLESSNESS

Most people rely on employment as a source of income. As of March 2018, the Scottish unemployment rate was 4.3%, with the UK figure at 4.2%. This figure has reduced: year-on-year since 2011–2012 when it was 8.1%.

Without a regular decent income people can find themselves living in poverty and struggling to pay bills and for the things they need.

However, some people cannot work because of health reasons, childcare issues or responsibilities such as being a carer for someone else. This is known as worklessness as they are not necessarily actively seeking employment.

Where people live may also affect their job prospects as some areas of the UK suffer from chronic unemployment and people get caught in a poverty cycle or the benefit trap, where working actually leaves people worse off. Statistics have shown a north/south divide in the UK, with unemployment and inequality higher in the north than in the south.

LOW PAY

Some jobs do not require specific training, skills or educational qualifications and as a result the pay may be very low. For example, the specific qualifications and training required to be the director of a major organisation mean directors can earn over £100,000 annually while a cleaner may earn less than £7000. This pay gap is on the basis of supply and demand. Those who have the skills most in demand are low in supply, meaning they can command higher wages than others.

Many employers now only offer part-time contracts for employees instead of full-time, significantly reducing the number of hours people can work and subsequently their pay. Those with childcare commitments have to face rising childcare costs reducing their income further. Despite the introduction of a **National Minimum Wage** (discussed later in this chapter) in 1998 many people in the UK still find themselves earning very low amounts, especially in comparison to those in roles that require very specific qualifications and training.

Low wages, part-time work and the high costs of childcare can result in low incomes.

Many low-wage jobs offer no chance of promotion ('low pay, low prospects'); others are insecure, providing only temporary and unpredictable incomes ('low pay, no pay'). As a result, they are often nothing more than poverty traps.

There are 1.4 million part-time workers wanting full-time work in the UK and 6.4 million people now lack the paid work they want.

The Government introduced a new mandatory National Living Wage (NLW) on 1st April 2016 to help the UK move towards '*a higher wage, lower tax, lower welfare society*' (GOV.UK). The current NLW, as of April 2018, is detailed in the table below

Year	25 and over	21 to 24	18 to 20	Under 18	Apprentice
2018	£7.83	£7.38	£5.90	£4.20	£3.70

(Source: Gov.UK)

BENEFITS SYSTEM

If a person is unemployed in the UK they may be reliant on **benefits** provided by the UK Government. However, benefits are deliberately set at low levels, leaving recipients living below the poverty line, and some of them are **means-tested**, meaning that the amounts paid can vary from person to person.

Some people may find themselves caught in the **benefit trap**, where it does not make financial sense to get a low-paid job as they will stop receiving essential benefits and may introduce new costs such as travel expenses and childcare.

In 2013 the UK Government introduced the Benefit Cap, which limited the total annual amount households were able to receive in benefits in order to encourage people caught in the poverty trap back to work.

GENDER AND RACE

Inequalities in gender and race are discussed in detail later in this chapter but it is important to address the fact that women and ethnic minorities have comparatively high poverty statistics.

Gender

Despite progress in this area women are still paid less than men (up to 15%), are less likely to work at all compared to men and can suffer from discrimination in the workplace. Some employers will view a male candidate for a job or promotion as less of a risk than a female as males are less likely to have family commitments and won't require lengthy maternity leave. This is known as the **glass ceiling effect** or gender stereotyping, where women can struggle for recognition and promotion.

Many women also find themselves in caring roles, limiting the hours and types of jobs they can do. This has an impact on their income, and many women will go without basic necessities to provide for others such as their children. Women are also more likely than men to be lone parents.

Race

The poverty rate for ethnic minorities is approximately 40% compared to 20% for whites in the UK. Many minority ethnic groups suffer discrimination in the workplace and may be overlooked for jobs and promotion.

Bangladeshis and Pakistanis statistically are more at risk of poverty than other ethnic groups.

FAMILY STRUCTURE

In 2018, almost 25% of households were headed by a lone parent. A lone-parent household may mean one income compared to a two-parent household with two. Lone parents are also less likely to work full-time or at all due to childcare restrictions, and may be totally reliant on state benefits for their income.

ONLINE TEST

Revise this topic online by clicking on the 'Causes of poverty' test online at www.brightredbooks.net/N5ModernStudies.

FACT

According to a 2017 study carried out by academics at Cardiff University, 60% of British people experiencing poverty live in a household where at least one person is working.

DON'T FORGET

There are always exceptions, e.g. not all lone-parent families live in poverty.

THINGS TO DO AND THINK ABOUT

1   Explain the difference between unemployment and worklessness.

2   Create a spider diagram of the main causes of poverty with brief summaries for each.

3   Why might some people consider themselves 'better off' receiving benefits from the UK Government than getting a low-paid job?

CONSEQUENCES OF POVERTY

ILL-HEALTH

Ill-health can affect those suffering from poverty both physically and mentally.

Depression

Thirty-one per cent of people in poverty reported having depression, while just 15.8% of people not in poverty reported having the condition. Depression is marked by dark moods, tiredness, thinking problems and trouble sleeping. Financial worries will have an effect on a person's mental state and how they will cope. Divorce is also more common in poverty, adding to the strain and onset of depression.

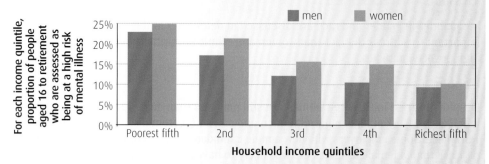

Adults in the poorest fifth of the population are much more likely to be at risk of developing a mental illness than those on average incomes.
Source: Health Survey for England, DH. Data are the average for 2008 and 2009, England, updated March 2011.

Asthma linked to poor housing

Children living in poor housing are almost twice as likely to suffer from poor health as other children. Low temperatures lower resistance to respiratory infections such as asthma. Damp in houses as a result of lack of heating leads to mould growth, which can also cause allergies. The most common cause of asthma in children is the house dust mite.

Asthma can be a terrifying experience for children. For some it can be a matter of life and death. But it's not only the physical problems of the illness that affect children. The illness will lead to increased absence from school and could have an impact on educational attainment.

Obesity and lack of exercise

Many stereotype the USA as a nation of obesity but new figures now show that on a 2017 OECD report the United Kingdom is now the sixth fattest country in Europe, experiencing a 92% rise in just over 20 years.

This table shows the distribution of obesity from the least to most deprived households in the UK:

	Least deprived	Second	Third	Fourth	Most deprived
Obese men (%)	22	23	24	24	25
Obese women (%)	19	25	28	28	30

This would lead people to believe that calorie intake must be higher in the most deprived groups, but a recent NHS study has disputed this. It found that the poorest 10% of UK households consume on average 1845 calories per day and the richest 10% of households consume 2009 calories. Food choices vary but the impact of no exercise seems to be key. Those in poverty are less likely to take exercise, which may be due to illness or financial strain, e.g. gym memberships are expensive.

FACT

The Joseph Rowntree Foundation estimates that poverty costs the UK £78bn per annum with key costs including £29bn on treating health conditions associated with poverty, £10bn on providing school initiatives aimed at supporting poorer students and £4bn on providing housing support..

HOMELESSNESS

Anyone can become homeless and many homeless people have previously had successful lives. Reasons for homelessness vary between males and females. The most common reasons for males are relationship breakdown, substance misuse and leaving an institution (prison, care, hospital etc.). For homeless women, the most common causes are physical or mental health problems and escaping a violent relationship. Poverty is a common theme amongst the various reasons given.

ADDICTION PROBLEMS

Smoking

Smoking is strongly linked to a stressful lifestyle and many use it as a coping mechanism. Around 15% of men and 14% of women smoke cigarettes in the upper and middle classes. This number trebles for working-class males to 45% and doubles to 33% for working-class women. In the most deprived groups, such as the homeless, smoking reaches 70%. Smoking 20 cigarettes a day costs approximately £3,800 per year. Those on a low income will be spending much of their disposable income on cigarettes and may be neglecting other important essentials such as heating and food, which will then have an impact on their health. The list of smoking-related illnesses includes emphysema, bronchitis, coronary artery disease, liver cancer, prostate cancer, erectile dysfunction in men, stomach cancer, bladder and kidney cancer, cataracts and cervical cancer. Those in poverty will be more likely to suffer from these diseases as a result of smoking.

Drugs and alcohol

Alcohol is another form of escapism and its consupmtion has doubled in the UK over the last 50 years. According to the NHS it kills at least 40 Scots a week. On the 1 May 2018, the Scottish Governemnt introduced a minimum unit price for alcohol in Scotland, which has been set at 50 pence. This applies to everywhere selling alcohol such as supermarkets, bars and restaurants. This minimum unit price was introduced in order to reduce alcohol consumption. According to Scotland's former Health Secretary, Shona Robison, 'With alcohol on sale today in some places at just 16 pence per unit, we have to tackle the scourge of cheap, high-strength drink that causes so much damage to so many families. This move will save thousands of lives.' Robison was replaced by Jeane Freeman in June 2018.

Research suggests that there is a strong association between poverty and problematic drug use. Those who are unemployed, particularly the long-term unemployed, and early school leavers have a higher rate of substance abuse. In 2016, 867 people in Scotland died as a result of drug use which was an increase of 106% from 2006. Heroin and opioids were responsible for almost 90% of these *fatalities* (*The Guardian, Tuesday 15th August 2017*). The worst figures were recorded in the most socially deprived areas.

Drug-related deaths in Scotland

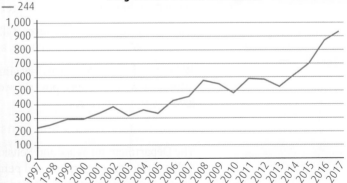

> 'Despite more than half a century of unequivocal evidence of the harmful effects of tobacco on health, today, one in every four men in the world is a daily smoker.'

Dr Emmanuela Gakidou – BBC News, 6th April 2017

> 'Smoking is the principal cause of the inequalities in death rates between rich and poor. Put simply, smoking is a public health disaster.'

Alan Milburn, former Secretary of State for Health

ONLINE

For more information about how smoking affects your health, visit www.brightredbooks.net/N5ModernStudies.

THINGS TO DO AND THINK ABOUT

Shona Robison believes that the introduction of a minimum unit price for alcohol in Scotland will 'save thousands of lives'. Which groups are likely to benefit most from its introduction?

ONLINE TEST

Check your knowledge of the consequences of poverty in the UK online at www.brightredbooks.net/N5ModernStudies.

TACKLING POVERTY

There are many groups and organisations that work to try to reduce poverty in the UK.

VIDEO LINK

Check out the video 'David Cameron launches the Big Society fund' at www.brightredbooks.net/N5ModernStudies.

ONLINE

Read more by following the 'Big Society' link at www.brightredbooks.net/N5ModernStudies.

ONLINE

Learn more by visiting the UK Government website at www.brightredbooks.net/N5ModernStudies.

UK GOVERNMENT

The welfare state

In 1942 the Beveridge Report was published highlighting the 'five giants standing in the way of social progress'. These five giants were *want, squalor, ignorance, disease* and *idleness*, and the report specifically focused on *want*, which today we refer to as poverty. The writer of the report, William Beveridge, believed that it was the government's responsibility to tackle these 'giants' and that a **welfare state** should be introduced to do so. The founding principles of the welfare state were that it should be collectivist (state funded), universal (free at the point of need), comprehensive (available for everyone) and equal (services provided to the same standard regardless of region). This 'from the cradle to the grave' Labour government welfare state provided a National Health Service, housing, education and employment programmes, and benefits all paid for via taxation and National Insurance in order to tackle poverty and its consequences.

The Big Society and Welfare to Work

The welfare state has changed since its implementation. People are living longer and the strain on the services provided by the UK Government has meant change was inevitable. The Big Society was the idea of former Prime Minister David Cameron. He believed in a more individualist approach to the welfare state and has made it clear that he wanted to replace some of the responsibilities of the government with increased control of more localised organisations and private companies. This has meant significant reform to the NHS and benefits system, and a movement towards achieving reduced welfare dependency.

UK legislation

Child Poverty Act 2010: The UK has set and aims to meet targets by 2020. The government will work alongside local authorities to assess specific needs and create strategies to meet them, but based on current statistics and the state of the UK economy it looks unlikely this target will be met.

Equality Act 2010: This law makes it illegal for anyone to be discriminated against on the basis of among others gender, race, age, disability or sexuality, especially in employment.

Welfare Reform Act 2012: This law aims to make the benefit system fairer and more affordable to help reduce poverty, worklessness and welfare dependency, and to reduce levels of fraud and error.

Department for Work and Pensions

The Department for Work and Pensions is responsible for administering the Welfare to Work reforms on benefits and pensions in the UK. The type and amount of benefits people receive is regularly checked and in 2013 significant changes began to come into effect.

There are many benefits that people can receive in order to tackle poverty. Many of them are means tested, meaning the amount can vary per person.

In 2013, benefits such as income support, child benefit and work tax credits began to be phased out and replaced by a new payment known as Universal Credit.

In 2013 a **Benefit cap** was introduced, limiting the total amount of money a household can receive in state benefits per week. The 2018 payments are as follows:

contd

- £384.62 for couples
- £384.62 for single parents
- £257.69 for single adults.

There will be some exceptions to this limit but these caps are intended to remove the benefits trap problem, where some people find themselves better off not working and claiming benefits.

Recently there have also been changes to entitlements for maternity and paternity pay, other benefits such as winter fuel and cold weather payments, grants towards improved heating and insulation, and maternity costs.

Benefit fraud and tax avoidance

Unfortunately there are people who claim benefits they are not entitled to and this is known as **benefit fraud**. The UK Government has reported that this costs £2 billion per year and was one of the main driving forces behind the Welfare Reform Act 2012.

Tax avoidance is when people don't pay the tax amount they should based on their earnings. This is legal but considered morally wrong as the people who do it tend to be very rich already! This costs the UK billions in tax each year and means less money can be spent on schemes like the welfare state. In recent times, many celebrities and high-profile companies have recently been accused of tax avoidance.

National minimum wage

The national minimum wage was introduced to tackle income inequality and remove poverty pay, but the rates (which vary according to age), remain low and some employers struggle to pay it.

Group	April 2018 rate
25 and over	£7.83
21–24	£7.38
18–20	£5.90
Under 18	£4.20
Apprentices	£3.70

THINGS TO DO AND THINK ABOUT

1. Explain the difference between the collectivist and individualist approach to the welfare state

2. Create a table highlighting the arguments for and against the national minimum wage.

3. Why has it been necessary for the welfare state to change so dramatically?

TACKLING POVERTY AND HEALTH INEQUALITIES

Learn more about the Child Poverty Action Group at www.brightredbooks.net/N5ModernStudies.

FACT

In 2016-17 there were over 1,100 food banks operating across the UK with over 400 of them being provided by the Trussell Trust.

DON'T FORGET

Social security and pensions are reserved matters currently under the control of the UK Government but the Scottish Government has the power to introduce legislation and set targets to tackle poverty and focus on groups at risk, e.g. The Housing (Scotland) Act 2001 set the target of eradicating fuel poverty in Scotland by 2016. Unfortunately, however, this target was not met and, according to the Scottish House Condition Survey, in 2016 183,000 households were found to be living in extreme fuel poverty.

FACT

In 2018, the charity Fare Share was given over £500,000 funding from the Scottish Government to help tackle period poverty, a cause championed by Labour MSP, Monica Lennon..

VIDEO LINK

Check out the 'Health inequalities' clip at www.brightredbooks.net/N5ModernStudies.

SCOTTISH GOVERNMENT AND LOCAL AUTHORITIES

Scottish Enterprise

Scottish Enterprise (www.scottish-enterprise.com) work with businesses across Scotland to stimulate economic growth and improve the business environment. They support businesses looking to expand and create jobs by offering loans, grants and expertise.

Scottish Development International

Scottish Development International (SDI) works with the Scottish Government and Scottish Enterprise to bring together resources and encourage companies, such as Mitsubishi and Morgan Stanley, to invest in Scotland and create employment opportunities for Scottish citizens. SDI's actions help to encourage Foreign Direct Investment (FDI).

Local authorities

The Child Poverty Act 2010 puts a duty on all local authorities to cooperate with central government and with each other to tackle child poverty. They are required to assess the needs of their local areas and create strategies to tackle specific problems.

Local authorities also provide free part-time nursery places for 3-year-olds to encourage parents back into employment, and Sure Start programmes provide support and training.

VOLUNTARY SECTOR

Local volunteers often work together to set up projects in their communities to tackle poverty and its consequences. They also lobby politicians for change.

Church Action on Poverty: Cranhill Development Trust in the east end of Glasgow, Save the Children, Barnardo's and Oxfam are all voluntary organisations that work across the UK to tackle poverty.

The Child Poverty Action Group lobby and campaign for better lives for low-income families.

DEVELOPING THE YOUNG WORKFORCE

The Scottish Government works alongside private businesses and a range of agencies to tackle Scotland's youth unemployment problem. Developing the Young Workforce (DYW) is a seven-year programme, which aims to reduce youth unemployment by 40% by 2021.

Renewable energy company Absolute Solar and Wind has been working with sheltered housing providers in Cumbernauld to install 96 solar panel systems on sheltered housing developments. This will help to reduce their energy bills and tackle **fuel poverty**.

LIFESTYLE

How people behave and treat their bodies daily has an impact on their overall health.

Smoking, alcohol and drugs

There is a clear link between smoking and health issues such as lung cancer. Drinking alcohol excessively can significantly damage your liver and abusing drugs can result in a number of health problems and addiction.

contd

Poor diet and obesity

What people eat or don't eat has a direct impact on their health. Eating large quantities of fatty and sugary food will not only result in weight gain and obesity but also has negative health implications, such as increasing the risk of heart disease.

Recent figures show that two-thirds of adults and a third of children in Scotland are now overweight, with the cost of obesity to society rising to almost £5bn a year.

Dr Andrew Fraser of the Royal College of Physicians in Edinburgh states: 'Obesity is a direct cause of a range of life-limiting and life-reducing illnesses, including a range of cancers, heart disease and diabetes. It means people cannot work, and is also a cause of very significant financial cost to a resource-limited NHS.'

Lack of exercise

Two-thirds of men and women are not doing enough physical activity to benefit their health. In Scotland around 2500 people per year die prematurely as a result of physical inactivity, according to government statistics.

GEOGRAPHY

Statistics have shown that Scots are unhealthier than other British people. They are more likely to suffer long-term illness, take less exercise, be overweight and spend more on cigarettes and alcohol. There is a clear north/south divide when it comes to the health of Britain, with Scotland and the north of England having higher death rates than the rest of the country. Scotland also has a higher rate of lung cancer.

Life expectancy figures 2014–2016

Area	Male	Female
Scotland	77.1	81.2
England	79.4	83.1
UK	79.1	82.8

According to 2014–2016 statistics Glasgow had the lowest life expectancy in Scotland for men (73.4) and women (78.8), West Dunbartonshire has the lowest life expectancy for women (78.8), while men in Perth and Kinross (79.9) and women in East Dunbartonshire and East Renfrewshire (83.5) are expected to live longest.

Three Cities Report 2013

This research, carried out by the Glasgow Centre for Population Health (GCPH), examined and compared the health and wellbeing of Glasgow, Liverpool and Manchester. The study aimed to explain Glasgow's reasons for 'excess' mortality (30% higher than the other cities) and the findings were published in June 2013.

ONLINE

Read more by following the GCPH link at www.brightredbooks.net/N5ModernStudies.

THINGS TO DO AND THINK ABOUT

1 Why might some families view the current child benefit means testing as unfair?

2 Using the internet and local media, research local projects in your area that tackle poverty. Create a leaflet/presentation to outline one of the projects, how it works and what it does.

3 Examine the life expectancy table.

  a What conclusion can be drawn about the area with the lowest life expectancy?

  b Why do you think this is?

ONLINE TEST

Test your knowledge of tackling poverty health inequalities at www.brightredbooks.net/N5ModernStudies.

TACKLING HEALTH INEQUALITIES 1

SOCIO-ECONOMIC DISADVANTAGES

Poverty affects where people live and their lifestyles. If you live in a run-down deprived community you're unlikely to go for a jog around your local area. Gym memberships can be expensive so people in deprived communities may not use health facilities even if they are nearby.

People on low incomes may be reliant on public transport, meaning they can't always travel to larger supermarkets and become reliant on the goods they can get from local shops, which aren't always fresh and healthy. Levels of obesity are often higher within poorer communities as a result.

People in deprived communities are more likely to suffer from depression and mental health problems. As a consequence they are more likely to smoke, drink alcohol excessively or take drugs as a release from their socio-economic disadvantages.

Sir Harry Burns, Chief Medical Officer for Scotland, has named this the 'biology of poverty'. He claims that a child born into the stress of poverty is negatively affected biologically and is more likely to succumb to ill-health than a child born elsewhere.

Social class

Social class is the category that people fall into based on their income and occupation. The lower down the social class scale you are the more likely you are to be living in poverty, and several government reports have highlighted the link between poverty and poor health. The World Health Organisation (WHO) published their findings of a 3-year health study in 2008, highlighting the effects of poverty on life expectancy. The report concluded by stating that 'social injustice is killing people on a grand scale'. For example, life expectancy can differ depending on the area you live in.

According to the World Health Organisation, men born in Glasgow have an average life expectancy of 54. By comparison, males born in close-by Lenzie are expected to live to 82 years of age.

FACT

Symptoms of deprivation include high levels of obesity, poor diet, little exercise, excessive alcohol consumption and drug misuse. *(BBC News, November 2016).*

VIDEO LINK

Learn more about social exclusion by watching the video at www. brightredbooks.net/ N5ModernStudies.

ENVIRONMENT

The environment that people live in can have an impact on overall health. This can be related to pollution in built-up cities or simply the household environment or family structure a person lives in. Unhealthy or abusive parents are more likely to have unhealthy children.

AGE

As people get older their health tends to deteriorate and they may require more healthcare and support. Conditions such as osteoporosis and diseases such as Alzheimer's are more common among the elderly.

GENDER

Statistically women live longer than men in the UK but they suffer more health problems throughout their lives.

The biggest killer of Scottish women is lung cancer and women have higher death rates from conditions as a result of ageing and mental health problems than men. Surveys have shown, however, that women are more likely to seek medical advice than men.

RACE

Ethnic minorities suffer from fewer diseases related to the overconsumption of alcohol and often have healthy diets compared to the overall population. This is directly related to cultural and religious beliefs, but ethnic minorities are more likely to live in poverty than whites and suffer overall poorer health as a result.

THE SCOTTISH PARLIAMENT

As health and law and order are devolved matters, the Scottish Parliament has responsibility for the NHS in Scotland and the introduction of new laws (legislation) related to health. The duty (tax) paid on alcohol and cigarettes rises almost annually and possession of drugs such as heroin carries heavy penalties.

Smoking legislation

In a bid to reduce the number of people who smoke in Scotland, especially young people, laws have been introduced to restrict smoking. Health warnings are now clearly given on cigarette packets to highlight the dangers of smoking and cigarette companies cannot publicly advertise their products.

Smoking, Health and Social Care (Scotland) Act 2005

- It has been illegal in Scotland to smoke in the majority of enclosed public places since 2006. England followed suit in 2007.
- In May 2016, the promotion of electronic cigarettes on popular forms of media such as TV, radio and internet were banned.

Tobacco and Primary Medical Services (Scotland) Act 2010

- People must be at least 18 years old to buy tobacco products.
- Tobacco products cannot be openly displayed in larger shops etc.
- Vending machines cannot sell tobacco products.
- Cigarettes can no longer be sold in packs of ten. This law came into effect on the 21 May 2017.

In December 2016, a new law was introduced in Scotland making it illegal to smoke in a car when a person under the age of 18 was present. Former Liberal Democrat MSP, Jim Hume, was an early advocate of the Smoking Prohibition (Children in Motor Vehicles) (Scotland) Act 2016 supported by organisations such as ASH Scotland and the British Lung Foundation.

In 2011, a Scottish study suggested that the air quality inside a smoker's car was comparable to industrial smog in cities such as Beijing or Moscow, even with the windows open.

THINGS TO DO AND THINK ABOUT

1 In May 2017, the UK Government followed the Scottish Government's lead in introducing plain cigarette packaging legislation. Why do you think the UK government may have initially delayed their plans to introduce plain packaging for cigarettes?
2 Why do you think women are more likely to seek medical help for health problems than men?

FACT

According to a 2017 National Records of Scotland (NRS) report, covering the period 2014–2016, the average life expectancy for females born and raised in East Dunbartonshire was 83.5 compared with 78.8 for females born and raised in West Dunbartonshire; a gap of 4.7 years.

DON'T FORGET

Health is a devolved matter in Scotland.

DON'T FORGET

Laws can vary in different parts of the UK as a result of devolution.

NO SMOKING

FACT

The Scottish government introduced plain cigarette packaging legislation in May 2016. This resulted in all packets of cigarettes displaying a graphic warning and using a standard size, font and colour.

ONLINE

Learn more about the smoking ban in Scotland at www.brightredbooks.net/N5ModernStudies.

TACKLING HEALTH INEQUALITIES 2

ALCOHOL LEGISLATION

Scotland has many health and crime problems directly related to alcohol and binge drinking so laws have been introduced to make access to alcohol, especially for young people, more difficult and expensive.

In May 2018, the Scottish Government introduced The Alcohol (Minimum Pricing) (Scotland) Act 2012, which was originally passed by MSPs in 2012. This is an attempt to improve Scotland's health, make it more difficult for young people to access alcohol and reduce the crime rate associated with alcohol.

Since 2010, the Scottish Government has banned cheap alcohol promotions such as 'happy hours' and charged some retailers a social responsibility fee for the damage caused to communities by binge drinking in pubs and nightclubs etc. Based on independent research, which looked at the impact across the NHS, police, social services, the economy and on families, the total annual cost of alcohol misuse is estimated at circa £3.6 bn.

NHS Scotland

- Free prescriptions were introduced in Scotland in 2011. This means everyone can access the medication they need regardless of income.
- In 2017, NHS Tayside's Quit4U programme which offered pregnant women grocery vouchers if they quit smoking was criticised for costing £485,547 in the 2015–16 period despite only encouraging 20% of participants (800 people) to quit smoking.
- Well woman and well man clinics offer free advice and support related to gender-specific health issues, e.g. prostate cancer checks for men.
- Free eye tests are available for all in Scotland.
- Free personal care is provided for the elderly in Scotland.

Working together for a healthier Scotland

The Equally Well Report was published by the Ministerial Task Force on Health Inequalities in 2008 and reviewed in 2010. It highlighted Scotland's health inequalities problem and set targets to reduce them and increase life expectancy. The Scottish Parliament has introduced several Scotland-wide initiatives since then to tackle health inequalities.

- Schools are encouraged to become health-promoting schools and there has been an increased allocation of PE time and more active learning within the core curriculum to get young people more active.
- Nutritional standards have been set for school meals with limits on salt and sugar content and pupils are given incentives to pick the healthier options at lunchtimes. Some schools think that packed lunches should be banned in schools altogether, and to limit access to unhealthier options such as fast food, an age limit has been set in Scotland on when pupils can leave school premises at lunchtimes. These plans are known as the Hungry for Success initiative.
- People are encouraged to drink more water, eat at least five portions of fruit or vegetables per day and drink alcohol 'responsibly'.
- Health and wellbeing is an important part of all aspects of the Curriculum for Excellence.

Some MSPs would like to prohibit food company advertising that targets young people and introduce laws that ensure fast-food restaurants, takeaways etc. are not permitted near schools.

VOLUNTARY SECTOR

Voluntary organisations work to improve specific health problems in local communities. They put pressure on the government to change laws.

- The Glasgow Association for Mental Health (GAMH) aims to support individuals suffering from mental health problems, which is now 25% of the Scottish population. GAMH provides tailored support covering a wide range of areas such as money and debt, employability and health and wellbeing.
- Voluntary Health Scotland is the national membership body for voluntary organisations working to improve health, tackle health inequalities or provide health care. They work with groups such as the Health and Social Care Alliance Scotland, Community Health Exchange, Community Food and Health Scotland, Voluntary Action Scotland, Scottish Healthy Living Alliance and Senscot.
- Oxfam carry out research and lobby the government on issues related to inequalities. They also support local organisations who work with vulnerable groups.
- The National Obesity Forum focuses on highlighting problems and tackling obesity from birth.
- UK-wide organisations such as the British Heart Foundation aim to highlight and tackle health inequalities.

LOCAL AUTHORITIES

The Local Government (Scotland) Act 1973 allows local authorities to introduce by-laws limiting the consumption of alcohol in public, for example with a few exceptions it is illegal to consume alcohol in a non-licensed public place within Glasgow City Council boundaries.

Scottish local authorities can provide free school meals for all Primary 1–3 pupils as well as free fruit and breakfast clubs to ensure a healthy breakfast, although recent financial cutbacks have threatened these programmes. Free school meals can be provided for some older children too.

Local authorities have responsibility for leisure services such as gyms, swimming pools and community centres. They often provide discounts for the use of facilities, especially for young people, to encourage more exercise.

DON'T FORGET

Community Planning Partnerships (CPPs) are responsible for bringing all the relevant organisations together locally and for taking the lead in tackling health inequalities.

PRIVATE SECTOR

The National Lottery has provided £300 million to set up healthy living centres in deprived areas of the UK to tackle issues such as heart disease, cancer and smoking.

Private health care and insurance

Some people choose to take out private health insurance policies with companies such as BMI Healthcare. Services covered can range from dentistry to surgery, but insurance policies can be very expensive. Some argue that due to the reduced demand, treatment can be quicker than on the NHS. The NHS have even paid for patients to be treated privately to reduce waiting lists!

Public–private partnership programmes

Under this initiative private companies build and run NHS hospitals on 'buy now pay later' schemes. In effect the government rents the buildings used as hospitals by the NHS. This has been a controversial programme as it results in paying back more than the project is worth over time. £6.7 billion has to be paid back over 30 years for 27 Scottish projects with an estimated value of only £1.28 billion.

FACT

Scotland's National Chef, Gary Maclean, regularly visits many of Scotland's primary schools to teach youngsters how to cook healthy meals and snacks at affordable prices.

ONLINE TEST

Test your knowledge of tackling health inequalities at www.brightredbooks.net/ N5ModernStudies.

THINGS TO DO AND THINK ABOUT

1 Outline the arguments for and against public–private partnership programmes.
2 Is your school a health-promoting school? How do you know?
3 Class debate: with NHS Tayside's Quit4U initiative costing almost half a million pounds to run but only encouraging 20% of its participants to quit smoking, do you feel the initiative should be extended to other parts of Scotland?

WEALTH INEQUALITIES IN GENDER AND RACE

DON'T FORGET

There are successful and independently wealthy women in the UK, for example **entrepreneurs** such as Dragon's Den star Deborah Meaden and Stagecoach co-founder Anne Gloag.

VIDEO LINK

Take a look at Labour MP Harriet Harman's CNN interview where she speaks in detail about 'breaking the glass ceiling' at www.brightredbooks.net/ N5ModernStudies

ONLINE

To find out more gender inequality from a UK perspective, have a look at the Fawcett Society's report 'Sex and Power 2018' at www.brightredbooks.net/ N5ModernStudies.

WEALTH INEQUALITIES AND GENDER

There are approximately 32.2 million women in the UK, which is more than the male population of 31 million, yet there is a clear economic division between the genders, with women 'worse off' than men.

- Despite more women than men being employed in education, health and social work they are still more than twice as likely to be paid less than their male colleagues.
- **Gender segregation** in the workplace is a key cause of the gender pay gap and there are roles in society that are considered female and roles considered male.
- Women are more likely to work part-time (74% of all part-time workers are women) and have more gaps in their employment than men.
- Women make up the most of those in low-paid work: almost two-thirds (63%) of those earning less than the National Minimum Wage are women. Women often cluster in roles relating to the five 'C's: caring, cashiering, catering, cleaning and clerical. These are often low-paid and temporary jobs.
- Women traditionally take on the role of primary care givers for children and that can have a significant impact on their income as they carry the burden of childcare costs, especially if they are lone parents (9 out of 10 lone parents are women). This is sometimes referred to as the 'motherhood penalty'.
- Women tend to be more dependent on welfare benefits than men.

The glass ceiling

This term refers to the invisible barrier that some women face in the workplace due to discrimination and stereotyping. Some women break through it but this glass ceiling can result in many women missing out on promotion and bonuses because of their commitments outside of work and prejudices inside work.

The glass ceiling exists when:

- Employers are reluctant to give positions of authority or responsibility to women as they fear they will not be committed enough or will take more time off than a male would.
- Women cannot compete for jobs with their male counterparts because they have taken career breaks or have gaps in their employment.
- Women cannot find successful female role models to look up to.
- A lack of flexibility in senior roles makes it difficult for women to juggle work and family life, e.g. no part-time work.
- Women cannot commit to the business life outside of the workplace and outwith normal working hours, e.g. on the golf course or in the pub.

In 2018 the BBC hit the headlines for failing to pay their male and female employees equally for doing the same job. According to former BBC Scotland health correspondent, Eleanor Bradford *'I was BBC Scotland's health correspondent from 2001 to 2016. I discovered I was one of the lowest paid correspondents at BBC Scotland, despite regularly appearing on UK-wide news and delivering exclusive stories. I regularly asked for a pay rise, and eventually cited equal pay legislation. This led to an immediate increase of £5,000 but it was not backdated. I remained around £10,000 below some male colleagues who were doing identical correspondent jobs. In one of my annual appraisals I was told I was a 'model correspondent'. I left the BBC.'* (BBC News, 30th January 2018)

contd

IN SCOTLAND WOMEN ARE

According to the Egender Sex and Power in Scotland 2017 report, women make up 52% of the Scottish population. Yet they only form:

- 35% of MSPs
- 26% of university principals
- 25% of company directors (in FTSE 100 companies)
- 20% of Major museums and galleries directors
- 16% of Council Leaders
- 0% of CEOs (in FTSE 100 companies)

- 28% of Public bodies chief executives
- 25% of Local Councillors
- 23% of sheriffs
- 17% of MEPs
- 14% of sports bodies CEOs
- 7% of senior police officers
- 0% of major newspaper editors.

WEALTH INEQUALITIES AND RACE

The term '**minority ethnic**' refers to those citizens who are not white. There is a UK population of roughly 5 million minority ethnics. This continues to rise, with the largest groups from Pakistani, Chinese, Indian and mixed backgrounds. Some areas of the UK have higher minority ethnic populations than others, e.g. London. Statistics show the following:

- There are more young black men unemployed than employed.
- Chinese graduates can expect to earn 25% less than their fellow white graduates.
- Those with an identifiably African- or Asian-origin name need to make nearly twice as many job applications to even get an interview for a job.
- There are higher rates of worklessness, unemployment and low pay within minority ethnic households.
- According to the Equality Outcomes and Mainstreaming Report 2013 there are 101 ethnic minority Scottish Government employees (representing only 1.61% of the total workforce).

The 2016 Joseph Rowntree Foundation report 'Poverty and Ethnicity: Key Messages for Scotland', highlights that 'Poverty is higher among ethnic minority groups than within the majority white population, but there is a lot of variation within and between groups and geographical areas'. Figures from 2011/12–2013/14 indicate that 20% of Asian and 31% of Black individuals are living in relative poverty.

Some inequalities exist for cultural reasons as there are high rates of lone parenthood within black African and black Caribbean communities, resulting in limited employment and reliance on benefits. Many Bangladeshi and Pakistani women are expected to stay at home rather than work or continue onto further education, which has an impact on household income. Some people from minority ethnic groups may be **first-generation immigrants**, which can result in language difficulties and qualifications not being recognised in the UK, limiting employment opportunities.

THINGS TO DO AND THINK ABOUT

1. Create a spider diagram of the factors relating to the glass ceiling effect for women.
2. Inequalities in race are more obvious in some areas of the UK than others. Why is this?
3. Think of the reasons these inequalities exist. Can you think of any new policies the government could introduce to tackle inequalities?

ONLINE

To find out more about gender inequality in Scotland, have a look at Engender's report 'Sex and Power in Scotland 2017' at www.brightredbooks.net/N5ModernStudies.

ONLINE

Check out the article 'Race inequalities exposed in public sector' at www.brightredbooks.net/N5ModernStudies.

DON'T FORGET

Not all people from minority ethnic groups live in poverty!

DON'T FORGET

Gender and race inequalities exist in health too.

FACT

One in four Pakistani men in Britain are taxi drivers or similar.

ONLINE TEST

Test your knowledge of this topic by taking the 'Wealth inequalities in gender and race' test at www.brightredbooks.net/N5ModernStudies.

TACKLING WEALTH INEQUALITIES IN GENDER AND RACE

GOVERNMENT RESPONSES TO WEALTH INEQUALITIES

The UK Government has introduced legislation and initiatives to tackle inequalities in gender and race, but the current Conservative government has been accused of not doing enough.

UK and European government responses

Previous laws such as the Equal Pay Act 1970, the Sex Discrimination Act 1975 and the Race Relations Act 1976 are now addressed under one piece of equal opportunities legislation.

The Equality Act 2010 makes it illegal to discriminate on the basis of:

- gender
- age
- disability
- sexual orientation
- pregnancy
- religion or belief
- race
- gender reassignment
- marriage and civil partnerships.

The Equality Act 2010 does not agree with the idea of different support for different social groups. It highlights the need to recognise that 'we are a nation of individuals', all with different needs and aspirations.

- The Equalities and Human Rights Commission (EHRC) has the job of trying to make sure the law works and promoting equality.

- In 2017, the UK Government's racial disparity audit highlighted 'significant differences in the life outcomes of British ethnic minorities and white people'. As a result, the Government launched a new 'Ethnicity facts and figures website' which provides data on a range of areas to help inform future policy making.

Scottish Government responses to wealth inequalities

The Scottish Government has introduced the public sector equality duty, which encourages Scottish local authorities to:

- remove discrimination and harassment
- encourage equal opportunities between different groups
- promote positive relations between different groups.

Since its opening in 1999 the Scottish Parliament has tried to remove the gender imbalance amongst MSPs by implementing standard working hours, holidays around school term times and crèche provision. This has only been successful to a certain extent as the role of an MSP can still be very demanding outwith office hours.

POSITIVE ACTION/DISCRIMINATION

Positive action is a UK-wide policy that allows employers to address an imbalance in their workforce. This policy aims to reduce inequalities and increase opportunities for women and ethnic minorities specifically, but does not mean that one candidate will be automatically preferred to another. Workplace audits may be carried out to check if imbalances have been addressed and it is not enough to simply have equal numbers of men and women, there must be a balance within roles, e.g. not only men in high-paid management roles.

For example, if two candidates with the same skills and qualifications apply for a job and one is from a minority group and the other isn't, then positive discrimination will ensure that the candidate from the minority group will be offered the job.

contd

FACT

Women-only shortlists for political representation are allowed until September 2030.

This is similar to American affirmative action programmes where employers are given quotas (specific numbers) they have to fill with people from ethnic minority backgrounds.

The Equality Act 2010 has not introduced quotas but some people are in favour of their introduction.

Nicola Sturgeon believes that a more balanced boardroom plays a key part in achieving economic growth. Speaking in 2015 she stated 'as part of wider efforts to reduce economic inequality, I set a challenge to all public, private and third-sector bodies to get a 50:50 gender split on boards by 2020. Yes, that's a target, and some may call it a quota, but how can anyone criticise efforts that seek to ensure that our public bodies and businesses use all of the talent available to them? It's good for society and, crucially, it's good for the economy.'

VOLUNTARY SECTOR RESPONSES TO WEALTH INEQUALITIES IN GENDER AND RACE

There are voluntary organisations that focus on highlighting inequalities and put pressure on the government for change.

The Fawcett Society

This is a campaigning organisation for women's equality and rights. They work to highlight and reduce gender inequalities in the UK.

The Joseph Rowntree Foundation

This organisation studies issues relating to poverty in the UK and publishes its findings on issues such as inequalities in race to encourage political debate.

Age UK

This voluntary organisation focuses on the needs of the elderly and highlights the specific needs of elderly minority groups.

THINGS TO DO AND THINK ABOUT

1 Outline the arguments for and against positive discrimination. Do you agree with this policy?

2 The Equality Act 2010 focuses on eliminating discrimination as a whole rather than on the specific issues such as gender and race. Why might some people disagree with this method of tackling inequalities?

3 Group investigation:

> Choose either gender or race.
> Choose either health or wealth inequalities.
> Create a **hypothesis** – what do you expect to find out?
> State at least two aims of your investigation.
> Investigate how your chosen group suffer from inequalities in the UK using at least two sources/research methods (internet, interviews, surveys, newspapers, TV programmes).
> Investigate specific groups and government policies that tackle your chosen inequality.
> Choose a method to present your findings, e.g. solo talk, group presentation, PowerPoint or poster.
> As other groups present their findings you should take notes.
> Finally, evaluate your investigation. How easy was it to find information? Were the sources you used appropriate? What might you have done differently?

ONLINE

Learn more about the Fawcett Society online (www.brightredbooks.net/N5ModernStudies).

VIDEO LINK

Learn more about the Joseph Rowntree Foundation online (www.brightredbooks.net/N5ModernStudies).

VIDEO LINK

Watch the 'Lunch clubs' clip at www.brightredbooks.net/N5ModernStudies to learn more about one of the schemes run by the Joseph Rowntree Foundation.

ONLINE

Learn more about Age UK online at www.brightredbooks.net/N5ModernStudies.

DON'T FORGET

There are many initiatives and programmes to tackle gender and race inequalities in health too.

ONLINE TEST

Test your knowledge of this topic by taking the 'Tackling wealth inequalities in gender and race' test at www.brightredbooks.net/N5ModernStudies.

WHAT IS CRIME?

Democratically elected MPs make laws that apply to the whole of the UK and since 1999 MSPs have had the power to make additional laws on devolved matters that only apply in Scotland, therefore a law may apply in Scotland, but not in England.

A crime is any act that breaks these laws.

ONLINE

Learn more about the Scottish Parliament online (www.brightredbooks.net/N5ModernStudies).

TYPES OF CRIME

In order to monitor crime statistics, the Scottish Government places crimes into two groups, property crime and violent crime. They then split crimes further into five categories. This allows the government to decide where to focus when trying to tackle crime.

Crime group	Definition	Number of crimes recorded by police in Scotland, 2016–17
Non-sexual crimes of violence	Murder, attempted murder, serious assault, robbery, other	7,164
Sexual offences	Rape, attempted rape, sexual assault, prostitution, other	10,822
Crimes of dishonesty	Housebreaking, theft, shoplifting, fraud, other	113,205
Fire raising, vandalism etc.	Deliberately setting fires and damaging property	52,514
Other	Handling a weapon, drugs offences, traffic crime, public disorder, other	54,946

Source: Recorded Crime in Scotland, 2016–17.

The Scottish Crime and Justice Survey (SCJS) measures recorded crime in Scotland annually. Their findings have shown that young males are the most likely social group to be victims of crime and that the crime rate is higher in areas of social deprivation, for example in Glasgow, with 96,791 crimes committed in 2016–17.

DON'T FORGET

These statistics are based on recorded crimes only but many crimes go unrecorded as people choose, for a variety of reasons, not to report them to the police.

ONLINE TEST

Test your knowledge of this topic by taking the 'What is crime?' test at www.brightredbooks.net/N5ModernStudies.

VIDEO LINK

Check out the clip 'Crime and public perception' at www.brightredbooks.net/N5ModernStudies.

On the 1 April 2013, all eight regional police forces merged to become Police Scotland. The organisation's purpose, according to their website, is to 'improve the safety and wellbeing of people, places and communities in Scotland' (*Police Scotland website*).

contd

Over the year, crime DOWN 3%

Lowest level
since 1974

238,651 crimes
recorded in 2016–17

No. of
crimes

1970s   1980s   1990s   2000s   2010s

Crimes tend to happen in larger cities, near to popular drinking areas and nightspots, and in socially deprived areas.

Serious organised crime

Serious organised crime can involve a range of activities from drug dealing and counterfeiting to prostitution and human trafficking, where vulnerable people are sold into forms of slavery. Organised crime groups can span the world and use the money they make from things like pirate DVDs to fund more serious crimes like human trafficking.

White-collar crime

The term 'white-collar crime' covers any crime that was committed for financial gain by 'a person of respectability and high social status in the course of his occupation'. Examples of white-collar crime are fraud, embezzlement, bribery, insider trading, money laundering and cyber crime.

Blue-collar crime

People in relatively unskilled occupations or who are unemployed and socially disadvantaged may commit crimes such as housebreaking, shoplifting or vandalism. These types of crimes tend to happen more often than white-collar crimes and are more obvious. They are known as blue-collar crimes.

New crime

As society and technology change, crimes change too. Crimes such as cyber bullying, where people are abused via the internet, and hate crimes, where people are targeted because of their race, religion or sexuality, have been on the increase recently. New laws have been introduced to tackle these crimes and try to prevent them.

 FACT

Since 2007–2008, some types of crime have increased, while others have fallen:

- Non-sexual crimes of violence are up by 6%
- Sexual crimes are up by 5%
- Crimes of dishonesty have decreased by 2%
- Fire-raising and vandalism have fallen by 3%
- Other crimes have decreased by 7%.

VIDEO LINK

Check out the video 'Mobile phone technology to help tackle crime' at www.brightredbooks.net/ N5ModernStudies.

 FACT

Teachers in Scotland are increasingly being subjected to cyber bullying from pupils. Sixty-eight per cent have received unpleasant e-mails, 26% have been the subject of abuse on websites and 28% have received abusive text messages.

THINGS TO DO AND THINK ABOUT

1   Why might some people not report crimes to the police?

2   What types of crimes are more likely to be committed by young people?

3   Explain the difference between blue- and white-collar crime.

4   Why does criminal law regularly have to be reviewed and updated?

CAUSES OF CRIME

It is not easy to explain why people commit crime as there are many causes. People have to be accountable for their actions, but it is clear that some people are more likely to commit crime than others.

INDIVIDUALIST VERSUS COLLECTIVIST THEORY

ONLINE

Check out the article 'What causes crime?' for more on this debate: www.brightredbooks.net/N5ModernStudies.

There are two main theories of why people commit crime. Individualists believe that a person chooses to commit a crime and they should be punished for it. They feel that stronger punishments would result in less crime. Collectivists believe that poor social conditions, such as poor housing and unemployment, cause crime. They feel that if people are employed and happy, they are unlikely to commit crime.

Individualists believe that crimes are committed based on a rational choice made by an individual, while collectivists believe that crime is a result of poor social circumstances that need to be addressed by the government.

POVERTY AND SOCIAL EXCLUSION

Local authorities with large cities and urban areas tend to have higher crime rates than more rural areas. Many of these areas are considered deprived and Glasgow City Council has more areas of deprivation than any other local authority in Scotland, as well as the highest crime rate of all council areas.

In some areas there is a lack of facilities, especially for young people. This can lead to boredom, which can lead to crime.

VIDEO LINK

Check out the clip 'Role of alcohol in crime', in which former Chief Constable of Police Scotland, Stephen House, discusses the issue

DRUGS AND ALCOHOL

In 2016–17, 77 people were accused of homicide (murder) in Scotland. Twenty-nine per cent were reported to have been drunk and/or under the influence of drugs at the time. Almost all female prisoners admitted to Cornton Vale prison test positive for drugs on admission. People who are addicted to drugs may commit further crimes to get access to them.

According to Homicide in Scotland 2016–17, over the past decade almost 60% of murders where the accused was suspected of being under the influence of alcohol occurred between Friday and Sunday..

GREED

Not all crimes are committed by those in poverty. Some crimes are committed by those from affluent backgrounds who want more money and think they can 'get away with it' and no-one will notice.

PEER PRESSURE

Many people, especially young people, feel pressure to 'fit in'. This may lead to people carrying out crimes they think might impress others or shoplifting items they cannot afford to buy, such as the latest mobile phone or gadget.

LACK OF POSITIVE ROLE MODELS

Some people may come from poor family backgrounds and have no positive role models in their lives to look up to. In some areas the people who are viewed as successful and influential are those who deal drugs or run gangs as few will go on to further education or embark on professional careers. Young people whose lives lack family structure may seek support from other places such as gangs. The gang becomes the family and they are often involved in crime.

Some young people may not be encouraged to attend school, meaning they have a lack of structure in their lives and a lack of opportunities later in life. Many children grow up in substance-abusing households. They are often neglected, which can cause long-term psychological and emotional damage. Many young offenders who come from 'troubled families' show a lack of empathy and can appear very angry. A lack of discipline in childhood can also be a factor and criminal parents often lead to their children to crime.

EDUCATION

It is often claimed that low literacy is related to unemployment, a lack of aspiration, poor physical and mental health, and/or great deprivation, which can lead to crime. Children who regularly truant or are excluded from school tend to have only basic literacy skills so it is thought that literacy improvement is a key part of any crime prevention strategy.

UK figures have shown that 25% of young offenders have reading skills below those of the average 7-year-old and 60% of the prison population have difficulties with basic literacy skills.

2011 ENGLISH RIOTS

In August 2011, a young black male named Mark Duggan was shot and killed by police in London. They had tried to arrest him and an illegal gun was found at the scene of the incident. Mark Duggan's family and supporters took to the streets to peacefully protest about the shooting but this soon escalated to full-scale rioting across several areas of London. Police found it difficult to deal with the increasingly violent crowds and the rioting spread to other UK cities such as Manchester.

When the riots eventually ended, five people had died, many people had lost their homes due to fires and businesses had been looted. The total cost of the riots is difficult to calculate but it is estimated at over half a billion pounds.

> *The Guardian* carried out a survey called 'Reading the Rioters'. They interviewed 270 rioters from ages 13 to 57 and from a range of ethnic backgrounds. Their findings showed that the majority of rioters interviewed were young males (only 21% females), poorer than the country at large, with low levels of educational attainment. Their ethnicities varied between areas and approximately 76% of those interviewed had previous convictions.
>
> Many of those interviewed stated issues such as unemployment, government budget cuts and recession, the growing divide between the rich and poor in the UK, and the lack of educational or entrepreneurial opportunities for young people, particularly those from ethnic minority groups, as reasons for participating in the 2011 riots. Others cited reasons such as retaliation against an institutionally racist and disrespectful police force.

THINGS TO DO AND THINK ABOUT

1 Create a spider diagram of the main causes of crime.

2 Carry out an investigation and present your findings on the causes of the 2011 riots.

VIDEO LINK

To find out about some of the successes of Police Scotland's Violence Reduction Unit (VRU) have a look at the video clip featuring John Carnochan at www.brightredbooks.net/N5ModernStudies

Commissioner Cressida Dick.

DON'T FORGET

It is important to remember that it is usually a combination of factors that leads to crime.

ONLINE TEST

How much do you know about the causes of crime? Take the test at www.brightredbooks.net/N5ModernStudies.

VIDEO LINK

Have a look at the news report on the riots at www.brightredbooks.net/N5ModernStudies.

FACT

In March 2018 Cressida Dick claimed social media applications such as Instagram and Snapchat were playing a huge role in 'soaring rates of knife crime in the UK'. (*The Independent,* 31st March 2018).

IMPACT OF CRIME

The Scottish Criminal Justice Survey (SCJS) states that 13.4% of adults over the age of 16 were victims of a crime between 2016 and 2017. This can be broken down to property crime (68%) and violent crime (32%).

Even crimes that are assumed to be victimless, such as tax avoidance, have a significant impact on communities as that money could have been spent to improve deprived areas.

WHY ARE SOME PEOPLE MORE LIKELY TO BECOME VICTIMS OF CRIME?

ONLINE

Check out the 'What is hate crime?' link at www.brightredbooks.net/N5ModernStudies.

VIDEO LINK

Watch the clip on stopping hate crime: www.brightredbooks.net/N5ModernStudies.

FACTFILE (based on 2016–17 SCJS)

- During the period 2016–17, property crime was recorded as follows: vandalism (34%), other household theft (27%), personal theft (26%), motor vehicle theft (8%) and housebreaking (5%).
- During the period 2016–17, the vast majority (72%) of violent crime was classified as minor assault with no/negligible injury.
- It is estimated that during this period, 57% of violent crime was not reported to the police.
- It is estimated that during this period, 15% of violent crime involved the presence or use of weapons.
- 23% of those surveyed felt community relations with police in their local area was poor.

Main findings on hate crime		
Crime types		Percentage of all hate crimes
Race hate	62,685	78%
Sexual orientation	9,157	11%
Religious hate	5,949	71%
Disability hate	5,558	1%
Transgender hate	1,248	2%

Source: Home Office Statistics, 2016–17, England & Wales

Please note, some crimes were recorded as having more than one motivating factor.

IMPACT ON INDIVIDUALS

The impact of crime on individuals can vary. Some people can seem fine whilst others have severe reactions. How people react can depend on:

- the type of crime committed and how 'serious' it was
- whether you know the person who committed the crime
- the support received from family, friends, the police etc
- personal history

Victims can struggle with the idea that a crime was committed deliberately by another person, unlike an accident, where there is no harm intended. Victims can feel powerless and vulnerable. This can be especially difficult to deal with if the crime is repeated or ongoing, which is often the case with domestic violence or racial harassment. It's also a big issue for hate crime victims who have been singled out because of who they are.

Physical

Victims who have been physically attacked may suffer scars or disabilities as a result. People can feel ill or be unable to sleep.

contd

When someone is murdered it is not just the victim who suffers, their families and friends do too.

Social and emotional

The social and emotional impact of crime or the fear of crime can be significant. People may become too scared to leave their homes, meaning they cannot work or attend school. People can become depressed or socially excluded and in some cases individuals can suffer from post-traumatic stress disorder.

Economic

Young people who commit crimes will have a criminal record for the rest of their lives and tend to do less well at school. This has an impact on their opportunities and job prospects later in life. People can lose money or belongings due to crime. Replacing items that have been stolen or damaged can be very expensive.

IMPACT ON COMMUNITIES

The broken window theory

This theory suggests that a broken window left unrepaired will make a building look uncared for or abandoned and soon attract vandals to break all the other windows. If areas are covered in graffiti and left damaged it sends a message that no-one cares and crime is acceptable, so crime rates will rise. Areas look run down and depressing with broken windows and graffiti so people will not want to live or work there. If an area looks run down, house values will fall, leaving people stuck in certain areas and creating derelict buildings.

Unemployment and lack of investment

If companies fear crime they are less likely to invest and create jobs in certain areas. These areas then become stereotyped and the cycle continues. This also means fewer local opportunities for young people.

Social exclusion

In crime blackspots people may feel unsafe and avoid socialising. This means no sense of community is created and people keep themselves to themselves. Gangs or young teams may instil fear of public spaces in some areas. This tends to happen in the most deprived areas.

Drug and alcohol abuse

If people feel depressed because of a lack of opportunities or a fear of crime they may abuse drugs or alcohol as they look for a distraction.

Increased police presence

Areas with high crime rates tend to have a significantly higher police presence than other areas as police try to tackle the issue. There may also be a large number of CCTV cameras, leading to people, especially youths, feeling they are not trusted and are targeted.

Increased security

In areas with high crime rates people may feel the need to take expensive security measures and prices may be increased in shops etc to cover the costs.

THINGS TO DO AND THINK ABOUT

Carry out a local crime survey in your area. You should aim to find out:
- what types of crime happen in your area
- why people think these particular crimes take place
- who is blamed for these crimes
- what can be done to tackle these crimes.

Think carefully about who and what you'll ask and be prepared to present your findings.

ONLINE

For more on the impact of crime on victims, check out the link at www.brightredbooks.net/N5ModernStudies.

VIDEO LINK

Learn more about the broken window theory by watching the clip at www.brightredbooks.net/N5ModernStudies.

ONLINE TEST

How much do you know about the impact of crime? Take the test at www.brightredbooks.net/N5ModernStudies.

DON'T FORGET

Many crimes that affect both individuals and communities are the result of anti-social behaviour.

FACT

According to the 2016–17 SCJS 77% of adults said they felt safe walking alone in their local area after dark. These results are the highest ever recorded by the SCJS. However, it is worth noting that over one fifth of those surveyed still feel unsafe which means there is still much work to be done.

TACKLING CRIME IN SCOTLAND

The Scottish Government is committed to making Scotland a safer place and believes strongly in crime prevention as well as tough sentencing. According to their bulletin, Homicide in Scotland, there were 64 victims of homicide recorded in 2016–17 (48 males and 26 females). This is a reduction of 44% across a ten-year period. There are various organisations in Scotland that aim to improve these statistics further.

ONLINE

Learn more about Police Scotland by viewing their website (www. brightredbooks.net/ N5ModernStudies).

POLICE SCOTLAND – SERVING A CHANGING SCOTLAND

In April 2013, eight Scottish police forces, the Scottish Organised Crime and Drug Enforcement Agency and the Association of Chief Police Officers in Scotland merged to create Police Scotland, which takes responsibility to protect the public and property, preserve order and prevent crimes taking place. Major crimes are investigated by the Specialist Crime Division.

Protect people and property	Arrest suspects, officers 'on the beat', interview suspects and witnesses, investigate crimes, stop and search
Preserve order	Presence at football matches, protests etc., community officers, managing traffic
Prevent crime	Work with community groups, visit schools, introduce initiatives, campus officers

FACT

Police Scotland
Purpose: improving the safety and wellbeing of people, places and communities in Scotland. Focus: keeping people safe. Values: integrity, fairness and respect

Some recent police initiatives include:

- Festive Domestic Abuse
- Cyber Fraud
- We can stop it (sexual consent / rape)
- Action Counters Terrorism (ACT)
- Be greater than a hater (Hate Crime)
- Child sexual exploitation campaign
- Safe summer
- Student safety
- Festival safety

Police Scotland has a network of armed response units across the country but the majority of officers only carry batons, CS spray and spit masks, and wear stab vests for protection. In 2017, the Police Federation launched their 'Protect the Protectors' campaign, which called for the introduction of body cameras, spit guards and tasers.

Policing 2026

'Policing 2026: Serving a Changing Scotland' was established by Police Scotland and the Scottish Police Authority (SPA) to help address the needs of Scottish communities and the changing demands of the police service. In 2017 an initial three-year plan was established, outlining plans to upgrade technology, invest in specialist cyber provision and introduce a new leadership strategy.

FACT

In June 2018, PC Laura Sayer and PC Kenny MacKenzie were stabbed in an early morning incident in Greenock, which some say has reaffirmed Police Scotland's decision to arm some officers with tasers.

ONLINE TEST

How much do you know about tackling crime in Scotland? Take the test at www.brightredbooks.net/ N5ModernStudies.

SCOTTISH GOVERNMENT INITIATIVES – SAFER SCOTLAND

The Scottish Government has set up several initiatives to promote Safer Scotland:

- Equally Safe – a delivery plan for Scotland's Strategy to Prevent Violence.
- Go Safe – Scotland's Road Safety Framework to 2020.
- CashBack for Communities – the Proceeds of Crime Act 2002 means the government can seize any assets it believes to have been gained though criminal activities. It then uses this money to fund community projects (aimed at young people) to prevent crime: Between 2008–2017, £92m has been allocated to a wide range of community initiatives in Scotland.
- Increased use of CCTV.

contd

COMMUNITY PROJECTS AND CHARITIES

Local councils, charities and communities often introduce initiatives to tackle particular crime issues in their areas.

- Family Action in Rogerfield and Easterhouse (FARE) – delivers an eight-week project to primary 7 pupils which raises awareness of the dangers and consequences of gang violence and anti-social behaviour.

- Medics against violence – volunteer healthcare professionals deliver anti-violence lessons in schools.

- Action for Children – Serious Organised Crime Early Intervention Service (Glasgow) which received a further £1m funding from Glasgow City Council in May 2018.

- Mentor Scotland – aims to stop children getting involved with drugs and alcohol by working with children, parents and policy makers (Edinburgh).

Glasgow City Council has introduced neighbourhood improvement volunteers, who aim to make communities safe and cleaner; graffiti teams and Nite Zones, which make it safer for those queuing for transportation such as taxis at night.

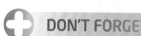

DON'T FORGET

Law and order is a devolved matter in Scotland.

CLOSED CIRCUIT TELEVISION

More than 4100 closed circuit television (CCTV) cameras monitor Scotland's cities and towns. However, the intense budget cuts experienced by Scottish local authorities in 2017–18 have led to some councils, such as Midlothian, ceasing to maintain public CCTV in a bid to save circa £30,000 per annum.

This has proven highly controversial, as closed-circuit cameras have been beneficial in solving serious crimes and tracing missing people. According to the *Daily Record*, antiterrorism experts warned against shutting down the network, as CCTV has been used to track down bombers. The leader of Midlothian Council, Derek Milligan, also confirmed that CCTV had helped keep down crime, especially in town centres, and that removing them would have a knock-on effect.

VIDEO LINK

Check out the arguments for and against the use of CCTV at www.brightredbooks.net/ N5ModernStudies.

KNIFE CRIME IN SCOTLAND

It is an offence to carry or purchase most types of knife in Scotland if you are under 18, yet historically Scotland had a serious knife crime problem, particularly when alcohol was involved.

Astonishingly, back in 2009–10 almost 50% of all murders committed in Scotland involved a sharp instrument. However, following the Scottish Government's successful 'No Knives, Better Lives' campaign, which worked alongside Police Scotland to tackle knife crime, Scotland has witnessed considerable success. In Glasgow, no children or teenagers were killed by a knife in the period 2011–16, a reduction of 15 from 2006–11. In 2012, the maximum sentence for carrying a knife was increased from four to five years. However, the average sentence for carrying a knife increased from four months in 2005–6 to 13 months in 2014–15. In February 2018, the Metropolitan Police Commissioner Cressida Dick visited Glasgow to meet the architects of Scotland's Violence Reduction Unit (VRU) in a bid to help reduce the number of knife fatalities in London.

VIDEO LINK

Have a look at the clips on knife crime at www. brightredbooks.net/ N5ModernStudies.

FACT

Statistics show that young men are more likely to be involved in knife crime than girls and that it is linked to **gang culture**. Gang members in Scottish cities like Glasgow and Edinburgh may carry knives to deliberately do harm to others, to protect themselves from rival gangs or because of peer pressure.

THINGS TO DO AND THINK ABOUT

1 Group task: Should the police be armed? Your group should research the issue, draw a conclusion and present your findings to the rest of the class.

2 'Increasing the number of CCTV cameras across Scotland would reduce crime.' Do you agree with this statement? Explain your answer.

ALCOHOL, DRUGS AND TRAFFIC LAWS

IMPACT OF ALCOHOL AND CRIME AND THE LAW

Alcohol has been shown to be a contributory factor in many crimes in Scotland and issues relating to alcohol (health issues, clear-ups, violence, etc.) cost the Scottish Government £727.1 million per year.

- In 42% of violent crime, the victim said the offender was under the influence of alcohol (SCJS, 2016–17).
- Over the decade 2006–07 to 2016–17, 42% of those accused of murder were under the influence of alcohol (Homicide in Scotland, 2016–17).
- Domestic violence incidents are often alcohol related.
- Three fifths of young offenders were drunk at the time of their offence (Prisoners Survey 2015 – Young People in Custody).
- There were 36,235 alcohol-related hospital stays in 2016–17.
- Alcohol harm costs Scotland £3.6bn a year in health, social care, crime, productive capacity and wider costs.

Source: Alcohol Focus Scotland

Anyone caught selling alcohol to or buying alcohol for someone under the age of 18 faces prosecution.

In May 2018 the Scottish Government finally managed to introduce the Alcohol (Minimum Pricing) (Scotland) Act. This requires a minimum price of 50p per unit of alcohol sold in Scotland. This is an attempt to improve Scotland's health and reduce the crime rate.

The Local Government (Scotland) Act 1973 means that local authorities can introduce by-laws specific to one area, e.g. it is illegal to drink outside in public in Glasgow but not in Edinburgh.

The Licensing (Scotland) Act 2005 came into force in 2009 and introduced laws to tackle underage drinking such as 'no proof, no sale' meaning if someone cannot prove they are over 18 with ID, such as a passport, the sale can be refused. In 2010 cheap alcohol promotions such as happy hours were banned in Scotland and venues selling alcohol now have a responsibility not to serve drunk people. Some alcohol retailers have been charged a social responsibility fee to cover the costs of alcohol misuse.

Police can take alcohol from underage drinkers in public places, and from those over 18 who are suspected of supplying alcohol to underage drinkers.

ONLINE

Check out the Alcohol Focus link for more: www.brightredbooks.net/N5ModernStudies.

DON'T FORGET

On the 1 May 2018, Scotland became the first country to set a minimum price per unit for alcohol. It is expected that other countries may follow suit.

Illegal drug classifications 2018 (selected)

Class A	Cocaine, heroin, ecstasy, LSD, magic mushrooms, methadone, crystal meth.
Class B	Cannabis, ketamine, amphetamines
Class C	Anabolic steroids, diazepam.

FACT

Cannabis was reclassified as a Class C drug in 2004 and reclassified back to a Class B drug in 2005.

IMPACT OF DRUGS ON CRIME AND THE LAW

Should cannabis be legalised? ✔ ✘

FOR	AGAINST
Some forms are stronger than others	Less harmful than alcohol or tobacco
Linked to mental illness	Dispute over link to mental illness
Gateway drug to harder drugs	Waste of police time

A total of 32,641 drug crimes were recorded in 2016–17, down from 35,479 in 2015–16. Drug crime in Scotland has decreased over the ten-year period between 2007–08 to 2016–17.

Penalties vary depending on the drug classification and the amount someone is in possession of. In the eyes of the law, dealing drugs is considered more serious than simply being in possession of some drugs.

contd

Drug possession crime in Scotland

- 86% of offenders from 2014–17 were male, with a median age of 29.

- For 2014–17, 42% of drug-related crimes involved cannabis; 18% involved cannabis resin; 10% involved diazepam; 10% involved cocaine and 8% involved heroin.

(Source: Scottish Government website)

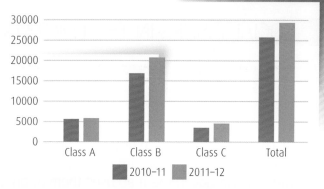

Number of drug seizures by Scottish police forces, by class of drug, for 2010–11 and 2011–12 (Scottish Government statistics).

SMOKING LAWS IN SCOTLAND

The Scottish Government is trying to improve Scotland's health by introducing tougher laws on smoking. This is targeted at stopping young people from taking up smoking.

Smoking, Health and Social Care (Scotland) Act 2005

- It is illegal in Scotland to smoke in the majority of enclosed public places.

Tobacco and Primary Medical Services (Scotland) Act 2010

- Must be at least 18 years old to buy tobacco products in Scotland.
- Tobacco products cannot be openly displayed in larger shops etc.
- Vending machines cannot sell tobacco products.
- Packs of ten cigarettes will be phased out. (This happened on the 21 May 2017).

THE ROAD TRAFFIC ACT 1988 (UK-WIDE)

This covers many aspects of driving and makes certain behaviours that are considered dangerous illegal. Under this legislation drivers must have valid licences and insurance, and wear seatbelts.

Driving under the influence

The Road Traffic Act states that the amount of alcohol a person can have in their bloodstream and legally drive is 80 mg per 100 ml. In Scotland, the limits changed in December 2014 to 50mg of alcohol per 100ml of blood. Driving under the influence of alcohol can lead to up to six months in prison or a fine of up to £5000, and anyone convicted of death by dangerous driving when under the influence of drugs faces a maximum sentence of 15 years. Police can now issue £100 on-the-spot fines for careless driving offences such as speeding, tailgating or not wearing a seatbelt whilst behind the wheel.

Speeding and totting up

Speeding is the most common traffic offence. The Road Traffic Act means drivers caught speeding will be given from three to six penalty points on their licence. In some cases, the driver can be disqualified from driving altogether. If a driver receives 12 or more points within three years they will be disqualified from driving for a minimum period of six months.

Using a mobile phone

Using a mobile phone whilst driving can result in six penalty points and a £200 fine.

Careless or dangerous driving

If a driver is charged with careless or dangerous driving they can be disqualified for a minimum period of one year and ordered to re-sit their driving test. A court can also impose large fines and even a prison sentence.

VIDEO LINK

Check out the clip on smoking legislation in Lanarkshire for more: www.brightredbooks.net/N5ModernStudies.

FACT

As well as removing the sale of cigarettes in packs of ten in May 2017, the UK Government also introduced mandatory plain packaging.

FACT

The Scotland Act 2012 gave the Scottish Government new powers over speed limits on Scottish roads.

ONLINE TEST

How much do you know about alcohol, drugs and traffic laws? Take the test at www.brightredbooks.net/N5ModernStudies.

THINGS TO DO AND THINK ABOUT

Class debate topics:
- Cannabis should be legalised.
- A zero alcohol limit for drivers should be introduced.
- The age limit for purchasing alcohol should be increased to 21.

THE COURT SYSTEM IN SCOTLAND

All courts in Scotland are organised by the Scottish Court Service (SCS), which is led by the Scottish Government. They deal with either criminal or civil cases. If someone is tried under criminal law, the Scottish Government accuses them of breaking a law of Scotland, whereas if a case is civil it involves a dispute between individuals or organisations.

DON'T FORGET

Scotland has its own court system, which is different from the rest of the UK.

The High Court of Justiciary.

ONLINE

Find out more about the court system in Scotland online at www.brightredbooks.net/N5ModernStudies.

FACT

The last person to be hanged for murder in Scotland was Henry John Burnett in Aberdeen on 15 August 1963.

VIDEO LINK

Check out the clips about the death penalty at www.brightredbooks.net/N5ModernStudies for more.

ONLINE

Have a look at the BBC Ethics guide on the death penalty for more: www.brightredbooks.net/N5ModernStudies.

PROSECUTION OF A CRIME

When someone is accused of a crime, the police submit the evidence to the Crown Office and Procurator Fiscal Service (COPFS), who decide whether or not to **prosecute**.

There are two types of criminal court procedure, solemn and summary. In solemn procedure a jury of 15 members of the public listen to the evidence and decide on the **verdict**. A judge is also present and he or she decides on any sentence that may be issued.

There are three main criminal courts in Scotland: the High Court of Justiciary, the Sheriff Court and Justice of the Peace Courts. Scotland also now has a Sheriff Appeal Court that can hear criminal appeals from the Sheriff Court.

THE HIGH COURT OF JUSTICIARY

This is the supreme criminal court in Scotland and it deals with the most serious crimes, such as murder (homicide), culpable homicide, rape, armed robbery, treason and serious sexual offences, particularly those involving children.

The High Court has unlimited sentencing powers such as 'life' (between 15 and 35 years) imprisonment or an unlimited fine. Prior to 1965, the High Court had the power to issue the death penalty (capital punishment). Those found guilty of murder would be hanged. The death penalty was officially abolished for murder in 1965 but it wasn't until 1998 that it was abolished for the crime of treason!

Arguments for the death penalty	Arguments against the death penalty
Current methods of execution such as lethal injections are reliable, quick and painless (more humane than in the past).	There have been instances where lethal injection has been slow and painful.
If a person takes someone's life they deserve to die.	Life in prison causes more suffering.
It acts as a deterrent to those who may commit serious crimes.	It does not act as a deterrent, for example the US state of Texas has executed over 550 people since the mid-1970s.
Some murderers are incapable of being rehabilitated.	It goes against basic human rights.
It costs the Scottish Government up to £40,000 per year to imprison one person. Life could mean 35 years, which is £1,400,000! That tax money could be better spent on other devolved matters such as healthcare.	Guilty verdicts can be wrong. Innocent people may be executed.

THE SHERIFF COURT

Currently, 39 Sheriff Courts represent districts in Scotland (this was formerly 49), and only 21 of these deal with solemn cases. These closures will also affect nine Justice of the Peace Courts that use the same facilities. Cases that would have been heard in these courts will be referred to remaining courts in other areas, e.g. Dingwall Sheriff Court cases will now be dealt with in Inverness and Cumbernauld Justice of the Peace business will now go to Coatbridge.

contd

Glasgow Sheriff Court deals with the highest number of cases in Scotland. This court hears both criminal and civil cases, and uses both solemn and summary procedure.

The Sheriff Court deals with crimes such as theft, assault, soliciting, possession of drugs and appeals from a Children's Hearing.

Under solemn procedure, sheriffs can issue sentences of up to 5 years in prison or an unlimited fine. Under summary procedure, a sheriff can fine someone up to £10,000 or sentence them to up to 12 months in prison.

There is also a range of **non-custodial sentences** that can be issued by the sheriff. These are addressed later in this book.

The types of civil cases the Sheriff Court can deal with are separation, divorce or dissolution of a civil partnership, adoption or custody.

JUSTICE OF THE PEACE COURTS

This court replaced the District Court in 2007 and is a lay court (business can be carried out anywhere) where a Justice of the Peace (JP) presides with the support of a legally qualified clerk. These courts deal with minor offences such as breach of the peace, being drunk and disorderly, and traffic offences.

A JP can issue a maximum **custodial sentence** of up to 60 days and a fine of up to £2500.

THE COURT OF SESSION

This is Scotland's supreme civil court and it sits in Edinburgh. The Court of Session can be used as a court of appeal and is headed by a Lord President. This court rejected an appeal brought by the Scotch Whisky Association and other wine and spirits producers against the Scottish Government's new alcohol minimum pricing legislation. The SWA then took this matter to the Supreme Court, and lost.

ONLINE

For more, check out the 'Scottish courts' link at www.brightredbooks.net/N5ModernStudies.

DON'T FORGET

The current Justice Secretary is Michael Matheson, who was appointed in late 2014.

ONLINE TEST

Test your knowledge by taking the 'The court system in Scotland' test at www.brightredbooks.net/N5ModernStudies.

THINGS TO DO AND THINK ABOUT

1 Explain the difference between summary and solemn procedure.

2 Create spider diagrams of the courts in Scotland. Include the types of case each court hears and examples of crimes, who is present throughout the case and the maximum sentencing powers.

3 The Scottish Government (led by the SNP) plan to reduce the number of Sheriff Courts in Scotland has been criticised by organisations like the Law Society of Scotland and political parties such as the Scottish Liberal Democrats and Scottish Labour.

   In pairs, discuss the issue and agree on the following:
   a   at least two reasons why the Scottish Government wishes to close these Sheriff Courts
   b   at least three reasons why other parties and organisations are against the closures.

4 Death penalty survey.
   a   Get into a group of three or four and create a survey of at least two questions based on the issue of the use of the death penalty, e.g. should the death penalty be an available sentence in Scotland for convicted murderers?

   Yes   No   Don't know

   b   Survey as many people as possible outside school and note their answers. Try to ask at least five different people.
   c   Collate your group's findings and present them in the form of a poster, using graphs and pie charts to display statistics.
   d   Finally, evaluate your survey:
      • Were the questions and people you asked appropriate?
      • State two good things and two bad things about using a survey for research.
      • Are there any other methods you could have used to find out information?
      • Might they have worked better?

VERDICTS AND SENTENCING IN SCOTLAND

VIDEO LINK

Watch this news clip about a famous not proven verdict: www.brightredbooks.net/N5ModernStudies.

ONLINE

Read the article "Not proven' fixture of Scots law set for review' at www.brightredbooks.net/N5ModernStudies.

DON'T FORGET

The not proven verdict only exists in Scotland.

ONLINE

Investigate the role of the not proven verdict in the trial of Francis Auld for the murder of Amanda Duffy in Hamilton in 1992 at www.brightredbooks.net/N5ModernStudies

FACT

In March 2011, the Double Jeopardy (Scotland) Act was introduced, which allowed a person to be re-tried for the same crime if there is 'compelling new evidence'.

VERDICTS

There are three verdicts/decisions available in Scottish courts.

Verdict	Definition
Not guilty	Based on the evidence the accused did not commit any crime and is free to go
Guilty	Based on the evidence the accused committed a crime 'beyond any reasonable doubt'
Not proven	There is suspicion of guilt but not enough evidence to convict – the accused is free to go

The not proven verdict is controversial as it suggests that there is some suspicion of guilt but the evidence provided does not prove guilt 'beyond all reasonable doubt'.

Arguments for not proven	Arguments against not proven
Allows judges and juries to express reasonable doubt	Evidence suggests guilt
Continues to be used in Scottish courts	May leave a permanent mark on the character of innocent people
It may be more satisfactory for victims and witnesses by reflecting the absence of necessary proof without casting doubt on their evidence	Traumatic for victims and families of victims
Juries can be unfairly influenced	Confusing and pointless

As Scotland has its own legal system it has its own range of sentences (punishments) that can be issued to those found guilty of crimes in Scottish courts.

ENTERING A PLEA

Before a case goes to trial the accused has the option of entering a **plea**. This means the accused can state whether they are guilty or not guilty of the crime or crimes they are accused of.

If the accused pleads guilty a trial is not necessary and the sentence issued may be more lenient than if a trial had gone ahead. The accused can also plead guilty at any time during a trial to try and reduce their sentence.

If the accused pleads not guilty then a trial will go ahead if the Procurator Fiscal feels it is necessary.

Barlinnie Prison.

CUSTODIAL SENTENCING

People accused of serious crimes may be sent to prison to await their trial. This is called being on remand.

If a person is found guilty of a serious crime they may be taken into custody. This means they may be forced to spend time in a prison or a young offenders' institution (discussed later in this book) run by the Scottish Prison Service (SPS). A judge can sentence someone to life in prison, which can mean anything between 13 and 35 years. At present, anyone convicted of a murder automatically receives a life sentence, with guidance to judges to impose a minimum 16-year punishment on those who kill with a knife.

If prisoners are well behaved, they may be given **parole** and released early or be given a non-custodial sentence for the remainder of their time. Some prisoners may be released on a life licence with conditions attached, which if broken will mean a return to prison.

NON-CUSTODIAL SENTENCING

Fine/compensation	Offenders must pay money, perhaps to the victim
Fixed Penalty Notice (FPN)	On-the-spot fines issued by the police for low-level crimes such as littering
Supervised Attendance Order (SAO)	Alternative to prison for those who cannot pay fines
Probation	Supervision for 6 months to 3 years, which may be combined with rehabilitation programmes
Community Service Order (CSO)	Requirement to carry out up to 300 hours of unpaid work in the community
Restriction of Liberty Order (RLO; electronic tagging)	Offenders are given a curfew and their movements are restricted for 12 hours a day. Offenders must wear a transmitter that alerts the police if they violate their agreed conditions
Drug Treatment and Testing Order (DTTO)	This is a rehabilitation-based sentence during which people are subjected to random drug testing and court reviews to monitor their withdrawal from drugs
Home detention curfew	Offenders must be in an agreed address by a certain time each day and if the curfew is broken they may be sent to prison
Community Reparation Order (CRO)	Offenders must complete up to 100 hours of unpaid work in the community
Antisocial Behaviour Order (ASBO)	This bans someone (over the age of 12) from causing disruption with their behaviour. ASBOs can be issued for crimes such as graffiti, noise pollution and littering. They are also used to try to keep people away from certain areas. Broken ASBOs can lead to fines or up to 5 years in prison.

Proposals for change

- More Supervised Bail Orders, reducing the number of people in jail before trial.
- More conditional sentences, with prison sentences imposed for not meeting conditions.
- Introduction of progress courts reviewing people on community sentences.

THINGS TO DO AND THINK ABOUT

1. Class debate: 'The not proven verdict should be abolished in Scotland.'
2. More non-custodial sentencing should be introduced in Scotland instead of prison.

   Do you agree or disagree with this statement? Explain your answer. Use the 'Rethinking crime and punishment' online link.

FACT

According to a 2017 report by the Prison Reform Trust, England and Wales has the highest imprisonment rate in western Europe at 145 per 100,000 of the population. Scotland ranks in second place with 138 per 100,000.

FACT

Ant McPartlin was fined £86,000 and disqualified from driving for 20 months in April 2018 after being involved in a crash where he was found to be more than twice the legal limit.

ONLINE TEST

Test your knowledge by taking the 'Verdicts and sentencing in Scotland' test at www.brightredbooks.net/N5ModernStudies.

ONLINE

Read 'Rethinking crime and punishment' and 'A unique punishment' at www.brightredbooks.net/N5ModernStudies.

THE SCOTTISH JUVENILE JUSTICE SYSTEM

YOUTH CRIME IN SCOTLAND

There were 1095 crimes among under-10s reported to police in 2011–12. Over 3200 crimes, including knife carrying, assault and sexual exposure, are alleged to have been committed by children under 10 in the past 3 years.

Strathclyde had the highest rate of reporting for child offending in Scotland in 2011-12, with police responding to 212 incidents. Two 8-year-olds were found carrying knives and two 9-year-olds were reported for a sexual assault on a girl in the region. Other alleged crimes include instances of breach of the peace, vandalism and racially aggravated conduct.

Under Scots law, children under the age of 8 are not held criminally responsible for their actions but can be referred to the Children's Hearing System on welfare grounds. However, the Age of Criminal Responsibility (Scotland) Bill is currently going through parliament with a view of increasing the age of responsibility from 8 to 12. Children between the ages of 9 and 12 can be dealt with for offending at children's hearings, while only those aged 12 and over can be prosecuted in court, if the offence is considered serious enough.

THE CHILDREN'S REPORTER

Scotland has its own justice system when dealing with people under 16 (and occasionally under 18). The system was implemented on the recommendation of the Kilbrandon Report and is part of the Children (Scotland) Act 1995. The Procurator Fiscal decides whether or not to prosecute and may refer children to the Children's Reporter.

The Children's Reporter receives referrals regarding children and decides if action is required. Referrals can be made by the police, social workers, health and education professionals, members of the public and even the children themselves. Offence referrals to the Children's Reporter fell by 3.3% between 2014–15 and 2015–16 to 15,329.

The Children's Reporter can arrange a hearing if they feel it may be necessary to introduce measures to support the child.

THE CHILDREN'S HEARING SYSTEM

The Children's Hearing System was introduced in 1971. Hearings are intended to support the child in an informal environment they feel comfortable in and they try to deal with the root causes of any problems. Hearings target both offending behaviour and welfare concerns, and aim to provide a safe environment for the child to discuss issues and problems.

The child is present at every meeting and they can bring a person of their choosing as well as their parents or guardians. Parents or guardians may be fined if they do not attend hearings, but in some cases they may be asked to leave the room if it makes the child more comfortable.

Meetings take place in the child's local area with three adult children's hearing members present. The panel must be made up of both men and women, and there are around 2500 people across Scotland who volunteer for this role. They are impartial and fully trained. Every Scottish local authority has a children's hearing panel.

A child may be placed before a hearing if they:

- are beyond the control of their parents or guardians
- are at risk of moral danger

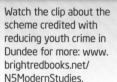

VIDEO LINK

Watch the 'Knife crime' animation for more on youth knife crime in Scotland: www.brightredbooks.net/N5ModernStudies.

VIDEO LINK

Watch the clip about the scheme credited with reducing youth crime in Dundee for more: www.brightredbooks.net/N5ModernStudies.

ONLINE

Find out more about the Scottish Children's Reporter online; www.brightredbooks.net/N5ModernStudies.

contd

- are the victim of an offence
- are likely to suffer serious harm
- are misusing drugs and/or alcohol or solvents
- have committed an offence
- are not attending school regularly without a reasonable excuse
- are subject to an ASBO.

What can hearings recommend?

The children's hearing panel can recommend discharging the referral because they feel that no action is needed. However, if action is required the panel can recommend that the child should be put under a compulsory supervision order (CSO). In most cases, the child will stay in their home and be placed under the supervision of a social worker who will be allocated specifically to them, but if a CSO is recommended, the child may be placed in care. This may mean they move in with relatives or foster carers, or into a children's home or secure accommodation. A CSO may limit who the child can associate with and force them into a rehabilitation or behaviour programme. Children's hearings can also restrict the movements of a child by issuing them with an electronic tag.

These requirements are reviewed at another hearing within a year. If a child or their family wish to appeal a decision made by a panel they can do so via the Sheriff Court within 21 days. A panel may also refer a case to the Sheriff Court if they are unsure how to proceed.

Strengths and criticisms of children's hearings

Strengths	Criticisms
More appropriate surroundings for young people	Slow to implement change
Children are active participants	Shortage of resources

YOUNG OFFENDERS

Young people can be sent to a young offenders' institution if they have been found guilty of crimes or whilst they are on **remand** and awaiting trial.

Prisoners take part in activities that educate, develop skills and personal qualities, and prepare them for life outside prison. They are also encouraged to exercise regularly.

Young offenders can undertake educational courses and gain qualifications in trades such as bricklaying and joinery. There is also a range of rehabilitation programmes and courses such as the Violence Prevention Programme (VPP).

Polmont Young Offenders' Institution (YOI) near Falkirk is Scotland's national holding facility for young male offenders aged between 16 and 21 years of age. Sentences range from 6 months to life and the average sentence length is between 2 and 4 years.

HMP (Her Majesty's Prison) Cornton Vale in Stirling houses female young offenders in Scotland.

Polmont Young Offenders' Institution.

 DON'T FORGET

The Children and Young People (Scotland) Bill was introduced in 2013 and may result in changes to the justice system.

FACT

During the period 2014-15, three in ten (28%) offenders in Scotland were reconvicted within a year. (*Reconviction Rates in Scotland: 2014-15 Offender Cohort*)

ONLINE TEST

Test your knowledge by taking the 'The Scottish juvenile justice system' test at www.brightredbooks.net/N5ModernStudies.

 ## THINGS TO DO AND THINK ABOUT

1 Why should a children's panel be made up of both men and women?
2 Why do you think the system was introduced?
3 Role-play how a children's hearing would be carried out.

SOCIAL ISSUES IN THE UNITED KINGDOM

SOURCE-BASED QUESTIONS: DECISION MAKING

These questions require you to use sources to make a decision about a given Social Issues topic. There is no right or wrong answer as you are only required to justify the decision you make. You will be given two options to choose from and must provide at least one reason why you rejected the other option.

Take the time to read the question carefully and analyse the sources before you make your decision. You must refer to all the sources provided at least once in your answer and you should show interaction between the sources, matching up written and statistical sources.

SAMPLE DECISION MAKING QUESTION

Study Sources 1, 2 and 3, then answer the question which follows.

You are an adviser to the Government. You have been asked to recommend whether the Government should increase the state pension age to 67 years.

SOURCE 1

Option 1	Option 2
The Government should increase the state pension age to 67 years.	The Government should not increase the state pension age to 67 years.

Facts and Viewpoints

The Government is considering increasing the age at which people can receive the state pension from 65 to 67 years.

- Life expectancy has risen considerably since pensions were first introduced; more people are living longer and claiming pensions for longer.

- The UK Government spent just over £44 bn on pensions in 2017; each year this figure continues to rise.

- If the pension age is increased to 68 years, approximately 2.6 million women and 2.3 million men in the UK will have to wait longer than expected to receive their state pension.

- There is a gap in life expectancy between men and women.

- Many believe that if people work longer it will help the economy as they will still be paying tax on their income and not claiming a pension.

- Due to the economic crisis, the Government needs to reduce its debt, which was over £1.78 bn in 2018.

- The National Audit Office estimated that £1.162 trillion was spent on bailing out the banks at various points between 2007 and 2011.

- Forcing people to work longer will mean fewer opportunities for young people getting into work.

SOURCE 2

Current pension age and planned pension age in selected European countries.

Country	Current Pension Age (years)	Planned Pension Age (years)
France	62-67	67
Germany	65	67
Italy	65 7 months	66 7 months
Greece	67	70
Austria	65 (male) 60 (female)	No change
Netherlands	65	67
UK	65	67

Survey Question: Do you agree with the Government's plans to increase the state pension age to 67 years for both men and women?

Yes	49%
No	40%
Don't Know	11%

SOURCE 3

Viewpoints

Giving people the opportunity to work longer is a positive step. Having a few extra years to add to your pension fund means a more financially secure retirement. It is unrealistic for anyone to expect that after working for 30-35 years the Government should then finance a 25-30 year retirement. Every year the amount of money paid out in pensions by the Government continues to rise. The Government simply cannot afford to continue paying out more money given the current financial situation. Every other European country is having to increase its pension age. Many workers have in the past been forced to retire against their will. Most people at 65 years would be happy to work for another few years.

Ross Dale

Increasing the age of retirement will be a disaster. When I started working I expected to work until I was 60 years old. As a woman I have already had to accept that I must work another five years and now the Government want to increase this further. People in Britain already work longer than many other European countries. I fear that I will actually work until the day I die. It is even worse for men who tend not to live as long as women. It is not possible for workers in some jobs to carry on until they are 67 years old. It is unfair to force people to carry on working in these jobs. Why should hardworking people be forced to pay for the economic crisis caused by the banks?

Mary Birch

You must decide which option to recommend, **either** increase the state pension age to 67 (**Option 1**) or not increase the state pension age to 67 (**Option 2**).

(i)   Using Sources 1, 2 and 3, state which option you would choose.
(ii) Give reasons to support your choice.
(iii) Explain why you did not choose the other option.
Your answer must be based on all three sources.

10 marks

HOW TO LAY OUT YOUR ANSWER

DON'T FORGET

Decision making questions will be assessed in the Social Issues unit of the course but may refer to any topic you have studied in the final exam.

Start by stating the option you have chosen. *(Outcome 1.1: Making a decision using between two and four sources of information.)*

> I have chosen Option 1; the Government should increase the state pension age to 67.

Justify your decision. You should provide reasons using evidence from the sources. *(Outcome 1.2: Justifying, in detail, a decision based on evidence from between two and four sources of information.)*

> One reason I chose Option 1 is because **Source 1** clearly states life expectancy has risen considerably since pensions were first introduced; more people are living longer and claiming pensions for longer. This is supported by **Source 2** which shows that Scottish life expectancy has increased significantly between 2010 and 2018 for both males and females. In 2010, female life expectancy was approximately 80 years and by 2041 this is expected to increase to approximately 86 years. Male life expectancy is expected to increase to approximately 83 by 2041.

> Another reason I chose Option 1 is because **Source 2** states that other European countries are planning to increase their state pension age. Germany plans to increase from 65 to 67 and France from 62 to 67. **Source 3** supports this by stating 'every other European country is having to increase its pension age'. The UK is part of the European Union and should try to have similar policies to other European countries.

> A final reason I chose Option 1 is because **Source 3** states that 'most people at 65 would be happy to work for another few years'. This is supported in **Source 1** which states that 'many people believe that if they work longer it will help the economy as they will still be paying tax on their income and not claiming a pension'. Therefore many British people would be happy to work longer and increase the state pension age to 67.

Using the Sources clearly state why you rejected the other Option. *(Outcome 1.3: Showing an awareness of alternative views.)*

> I did not choose Option 2 (do not increase the pension age) as although in **Source 3** Mary Birch says 'why should hardworking people be forced to pay for the economic crisis caused by the banks', **Source 1** states that due to the economic crisis, the Government needs to reduce its spending and debt, which was over £1.78 trillion in 2018 and **Source 2** shows that 49% of people asked if they agreed with the Government's plans to increase the state pension age to 67 said yes which was the highest percentage. 40% said no and 11% said they didn't know.

INTERNATIONAL ISSUES

INTERNATIONAL ISSUES: AN OVERVIEW

In this unit we will be learning about different countries and international issues. These countries and issues are linked to Scotland and have an impact on our lives.

WORLD POWERS

This topic will investigate three countries: Brazil (pages 86–89), India (pages 90–95) and the USA (pages 96–101). We will look into the political system of each of these countries, and the social and economic issues that exist there.

We should learn about these countries because of their international influence.

The USA is the wealthiest country in the world and is home to countless companies that operate in many countries, including the UK, for example Apple and Nike. Although Brazil and India are not as powerful as the USA they have been identified as growing countries that are becoming more powerful. As a result of their rapidly expanding economies and increasing participation in international issues they are part of the **BRICS** nations.

We should also learn about these countries because they are linked to the UK through international organisations such as the G20, the UN and NATO. Through these organisations these countries work with each other to tackle international issues.

G20

The Group of Twenty (**G20**) is an international alliance of 19 countries and the European Union (EU) that was created in 1999. They work together to devise strategies to improve the world's economy and aim to make it as stable as possible. These countries are very powerful, for example combined they account for 90% of global GDP and 80% of international trade. They are also home to two-thirds of the world's population.

Members: Argentina, Australia, Brazil, Canada, China, the EU, France, Germany, India, Indonesia, Italy, Japan, Mexico, Republic of Korea, Russia, Saudi Arabia, South Africa, Turkey, the United Kingdom and the USA.

UN

The UN is an international organisation dedicated to promoting security, social progress and human rights throughout the world. There are currently 193 UN members, who are working toward a range of goals and aims to improve the lives of millions of people. The USA, like the UK, has a permanent seat on the UN Security Council. This position allows them to veto international action discussed by the UN.

NATO

The North Atlantic Treaty Organisation (NATO) is made up of 29 countries that work together to ensure peace and security. The organisation has been involved in many international conflicts, including the wars in Bosnia and Afghanistan.

Members: Albania, Belgium, Bulgaria, Canada, Croatia, Czech Republic, Denmark, Estonia, France, Germany, Greece, Hungary, Iceland, Italy, Latvia, Lithuania, Luxembourg, Montenegro, the Netherlands, Norway, Poland, Portugal, Romania, Slovakia, Slovenia, Spain, Turkey, the UK and the USA.

WORLD ISSUES

In this topic we are going to explore three international issues: **human rights** (pages 102–107), child soldiers (pages 110–113) and international inequalities (pages 114–121). We will examine the cause and impacts of each of the issues and assess the attempts to resolve them.

Human rights

Not all countries have the same level of human rights that we do here in the UK. The UK is committed to promoting and defending human rights across the world. Being part of international organisations such as the UN and international pressure groups, and supporting local campaigns achieve this.

By using Libya as a case study we can discover the ways in which the international community can intervene when human rights are being denied by a government on a national scale.

The international pressure group Amnesty International is an example of how charity organisations can actively promote and improve human rights. We will look at the use of the death penalty as an example of this.

Local people are also able to make a difference in individual human rights cases. By exploring women's rights in Afghanistan we can compare life in Afghanistan to life in the UK and discover the ways that people are trying to change their own situation. We will also study the case of Pussy Riot in Russia, where the government is accused of not permitting as much freedom of expression as we experience in the UK.

Child soldiers

As part of the international community that condemns the use of children in war the UK is part of resolutions to stop child soldiers. The UK's army and non-government groups are also restricted by international law as to who can fill their ranks. Without these laws life for children in Scotland could be very different.

This section outlines the laws in place to protect children and the problems that exist with regard to these laws. We will then go on to learn about what life is like for children who become soldiers and what action has been taken to help them.

International inequality

Not everyone has access to basic requirements such as food, health care or education. These are aspects of life that here in the UK we can take for granted. The international community has acknowledged these inequalities and has made a commitment to work together to reduce them.

As part of this commitment eight **Millennium Development Goals** were created:

1   Eradicate extreme poverty and hunger.

2   Achieve universal primary education.

3   Promote gender equality and empower women.

4   Reduce child mortality.

5   Improve maternal health.

6   Combat HIV/AIDS, malaria and other diseases.

7   Ensure environmental sustainability.

8   Set up global partnership of development.

The UK is part of the group working towards achieving these goals. We will study three of the areas: world hunger, education and child mortality.

WORLD POWER: BRAZIL

BRAZIL'S POLITICAL SYSTEM

In Brazil there is one government that has authority over the whole country and separate states with specific powers, this is known as a federal government. The current constitution was created in 1988 and was the country's turning point from military dictatorship to a democratic system of government. Since its creation it has had over 30 amendments.

FEDERAL GOVERNMENT: EXECUTIVE BRANCH (THE UNION)

The executive branch of the Brazilian government is made up of a Cabinet of ministers for each executive area and is headed by the president and the vice-president. In 2010 Brazil gained its first female president: Dilma Rousseff. However, she was impeached in 2016 for breaking budgetary laws. Rousseff's successor is Brazil's current President Michel Temer. Women are historically under-represented in the Cabinet, but Rousseff's Cabinet contained a record number of female ministers (10, 26%).

To become president the candidate has to win an outright majority in the first set of elections. If this is not achieved then the first and second candidates must have a run-off election to determine the winner.

PROFILE: MICHEL TEMER (37TH PRESIDENT)

Born	1940
Party	Brazilian Democratic Movement
Previous positions	Vice President (2011–16), President of the Chamber of Deputies (1997–98, 1999–2000, 2009–10
Background	Supported an underground resistance to the 1964 military dictatorship, resulting in her being jailed for 3 years
Education	Law
Powers	• Outlined in Article 21 of the Constitution • Command armed forces • Appoint commanders of the forces • Appoint a range of senior officials, including the Supreme Court Ministers and the President of the Central Bank (Note: These appointments have to be approved by Congress) • With approval of Congress, declare war • Plan the budget • Veto laws suggested by Congress • Propose laws to Congress

PRESIDENTIAL ELECTIONS 2014

The next Brazilian General Elections are due to take place in October 2018.

2014 Election results

First round

Dilma Rousseff (Workers' Party): 41.59% (43,267,668)
Aécio Neves (Social Democratic Party): 33.55% (34,897,211)
Marina Silva (Sustainability Party): 21.32% (22,176,619)

Second round

Dilma Rousseff: 51.64 (54,501,119)
Aécio Neves: 48.36 (51,041,155)

FEDERAL GOVERNMENT: LEGISLATIVE BRANCH

The National Congress is the legislative branch of the Brazilian Government and contains two houses: the Chamber of Deputies and the Federal Senate.

House	Seats	Voting system	Term
Chamber of Deputies	513 Each state and the federal district have representatives based on the size of its population Minimum of eight and maximum of 70 deputies allowed per state	List system (proportional representation)	4 years
Federal Senate	81 Three per state and the federal district	FPTP	8 years

It is the National Congress's role to pass new laws, and both the Chamber and the Senate must pass every law. They also have the power to authorise the president to declare war.

JUDICIAL BRANCH

The role of the judicial branch is to protect the rights of citizens and ensure the constitution is upheld. The Supreme Federal Court is the highest court in Brazil and comprises 11 ministers that are chosen by the president and approved by the Senate. Cases can be appealed to the Supreme Federal Court from the lower courts and as a result the court has an extensive workload.

STATE GOVERNMENT

There are 26 states and one federal district, where the capital, Brasilia, is located. Each state has its own government and set of powers. Any power that is not enshrined in federal law belongs to the states. The governor and legislative assembly in each state have power over local state issues such as policing and the criminal justice system. They also work with the federal government to provide health and education. Elections are held every 4 years.

MUNICIPALITIES

Brazil is divided further into over 5500 separate municipalities that deal with local council issues. Each area covers on average 35,000 residents and states have around 214 municipalities each. The municipalities can pass laws on local issues and are headed by an elected mayor.

ELECTRONIC VOTING

Electronic voting was first introduced in Brazil in 1996. It didn't take long to develop and by 2000 all votes were cast this way. The government claims that this makes the process easier for citizens and reduces the number of mistakes. Each candidate is allocated a number and voters select their choice. The computer also shows the picture of each of the candidates to ensure they are making the correct numerical selection. It takes just 6 hours to count the votes! In June 2018, in what was a highly controversial decision, Brazil's Supreme Court ruled that no paper ballots would be permitted in the 2018 elections.

PRESSURE GROUPS

Landless Workers' Movement

- 1.5 million members in 23 of 27 states.
- Campaigns for the distribution of unused land.
- Built farms, houses and schools on the land they have gained.

Central Unica dos Trabalhadores

- Highly influential trade union.
- Represents over 7.4 million workers.
- Campaigns to improve the rights of workers.

FACT

Voting is compulsory for citizens aged between 18 and 70.

FACT

If the president or vice-president wish to leave Brazil for more than 15 days they have to gain permission from the National Congress.

DON'T FORGET

You should use Brazilian examples in your answers.

ONLINE

Check out the Brazilian government website for research at www.brightredbooks.net/N5ModernStudies.

ONLINE TEST

Take the 'Brazil's political system' test online at www.brightredbooks.net/N5ModernStudies.

THINGS TO DO AND THINK ABOUT

1 Create a diagram showing the structure of Brazil's political system.
2 What problem is there within Brazilian politics? Has this ever happened in the UK?
3 Does Brazil use any voting systems that are used in the UK?
4 In what ways can Brazilian citizens participate in politics?

INEQUALITIES IN BRAZIL: DRUGS AND POVERTY

BRAZIL'S DRUG PROBLEM

Recent studies have revealed that there are around 1–1.2 million crack users in Brazil, making it the second largest consumer of cocaine in the world. Brazil has had problems with cocaine since the 1990s, but recently there has been an increase in demand for both powder cocaine and crack.

Traffickers pay $50/kg and cocaine is shipped to Porto Velho for $250/kg, then sold for $6000/kg in Sao Paulo.

President Lula, took a different approach to drug abuse and viewed the issue as a health problem. As a result he changed the law and people who possess or use drugs are no longer arrested or imprisoned. Instead they are issued with fines or put on community service and/or treatment programmes. However, it is very difficult to split those who are selling and those who are using the drugs themselves. This means that there are still large numbers of people being imprisoned. There has been so much controversy over the large number of imprisonments that an interest group called Drug Law: It's Time to Change has emerged.

President Michel Temer has also focused on dealing with Brazil's drug and gang problem:

- Army presence in Rio during major sporting events such as the Olympics and World Cup, with the army assuming responsibility for leading the police.

- Border patrol with Columbia to prevent drugs making their way to criminal gangs. The President has vowed to 'improve military surveillance'.

- Improved intelligence sharing with nations like Columbia and Peru

CITY CASE STUDY: DRUGS IN SAO PAULO

Sao Paulo, the largest city in Brazil, has experienced problems with drugs for a long time. The area where there are large numbers of drug users and dealers has been renamed 'Cracolandia', meaning 'Crackland'. Throughout the past two decades the streets in this area have been inundated with an estimated 2000 users. This has had a devastating impact on the area. Law-abiding citizens have moved away, businesses have to shut early in the evening and rent has become very cheap. Although there is an official population of around 12,000 there are no childcare, education or health systems. Rubbish is also a major factor, with drug users and squatters scavenging for food.

Dor e Sofrimento (Pain and Suffering)

Local authorities have tried to redistribute the street addicts into different areas in order to break up the high population. Authorities discovered that this tactic didn't deal with the long-term problem but just increased the number of areas affected by drugs.

Drug-treatment centres

Some authorities have required addicts to attend drug-treatment centres. A very popular centre called CRATOD is located in Parque da Luz, near Cracolando. Addicts can attend drop-in sessions and receive the support and advice they need. Many people will volunteer to attend these centres, but the drop-out rate is very high on long-term programmes. Although the centres can help there are very few of them and they are overwhelmed by the number of people needing support.

POVERTY IN BRAZIL

- Poverty line: R$387.07 per month (family income).
- Approximately 25% of the population (50 m people) living below this line according to the Brazilian Institute of Geography and Statistics (IBGE).

Brazil is a country of great inequality and there is a vast gap between the rich and the poor. According to a 2017 Oxfam report 'The Distance that Unites Us', Brazil's six wealthiest citizens have the same wealth as almost half of the country's total population (100m Brazilians). Significant income inequality also exists between white Brazilians and those who are black or mixed race. The Workers' Party has made tackling poverty a key issue and both President Lula and President Rousseff have made a positive impact.

When President Lula was in power between 2003 and 2011, household income increased by 27%. Unemployment rates also improved, with a decrease from 9.1% in 2002 to 6.8% in 2011. When President Rousseff took over from Lula she made the promise to eliminate extreme poverty in the duration of her term.

President Lula

Consolidated the previous government's welfare policies and increased funding:

- 'Bolsa Famila' – part of Lula's 'Fome Zero' initiative to ensure that every Brazilian has enough food to eat.
- Money for mothers who send their children to school.
- A special credit card for buying food.
- Financial support to purchase gas cylinders.
- Consolidated welfare recipient list.
- Funding increase from R$2.4 billion in 2002 to R$8.3 billion in 2006.

President Rousseff

'Extreme poverty in Brazil will soon become extinct.' (Rousseff, 2013.)

'Brasil Sem Miseria' (Brazil Without Misery).

When President Rousseff first came to power in 2011 she added another 2.8 million people to the welfare list and helped an extra 22 million out of extreme poverty by giving them extra cash benefits.

- *Bolsa Familia*: a programme originally for children under the age of 15 to ensure that income per person was R$70, but now extended to include any family receiving social welfare.
- *Busca Ativa* (Active Search): this policy was created to meet the needs of poor people who lived in rural and isolated areas of Brazil. Rousseff believes there are about 2.5 million people who do not receive benefits they are entitled to because they live in isolated areas and lack the required information.

President Temer

- Brazil experiencing severe recession from 2016 onwards.
- Unemployment rate of circa 12.9% (April 2018).
- Temer has decided to cut spending on social programmes due to finding fraudulent claims from poorest in society.
- World Bank estimates that up to 3.6m could have fallen back into poverty between 2016–17.

ONLINE

Head to the Digital Zone to find out about President Temer being charged with corruption.

DON'T FORGET

Make sure you always explain how the government's policies help meet the needs of people.

FACT

In February 2018, Temer announced that he wished to scrap the Bolsa Familia scheme which costs the Brazilian Government approximately $8bn per annum. This scheme has played a vital role in reducing poverty in the country over the past decade.

ONLINE TEST

Take the 'Inequalities in Brazil' test online at www.brightredbooks.net/N5ModernStudies.

THINGS TO DO AND THINK ABOUT

1. Make a list of all the problems that drug addiction causes. Consider the impact on the local area, families, the individual and the government.
2. Despite years of improvements under Lula and Rousseff, what evidence is there to suggest that poverty within Brazil is now increasing?

INEQUALITIES IN BRAZIL: HOUSING AND THE RAINFOREST

CASE STUDY: CITY SLUMS

As the population in Brazil's cities has grown so has the problem of inadequate housing. Rio and Sao Paulo are particularly expensive places to live. Housing prices have rocketed in recent times as the nation has hosted two major sporting events in the past few years – the 2014 World Cup and the 2016 Olympic Games. Despite this there is a shortage of 8 million houses, with 50 million people living in poor housing. Over 24 million people in city areas don't have access to drinking water, and 83 million homes do not have an adequate sewage system. Poor areas in the city are known as slums or **favelas**.

Rio

Drug gangs, who have had full control of the slum areas, have dominated the city of Rio. However, the government has made a huge effort to overthrow the drug gangs and take back these areas. Since 2011 the authorities have removed drug gangs from many favelas and regenerated these areas. This process is referred to as 'slum pacification' and was put in place in order to help the city prepare for the 2014 World Cup and 2016 Olympics. As a result of this process crime has decreased, with murder rates dropping, and the areas are now viewed as a great real estate investment.

FACT

BRICS nations are the emerging powerful economy countries: Brazil, Russia, India, China and South Africa.

DON'T FORGET

People living in Brazilian favelas have a life expectancy circa 20 years below the national average at 48 years.

FACT

The Amazon rainforest produces over 20% of the world's oxygen.

BRAZIL'S ECONOMY

Brazil is the most powerful South American country and is one of the BRICS nations. Brazil is currently the eighth-largest economy in the world. The economy is based on the agriculture, mining and service sectors.

Despite a prosperous period prior to 2016, Brazil is currently recovering from one of the worst recessions in the country's history when the Brazilian real was weakened as a result of falling commodity prices and a decrease in exports. In 2017, Brazilian GDP per capita was $9,895.

Farming

Brazil has been very successful with farming for sugar cane, coffee and tropical fruits, and is currently the world's biggest producer of these goods. The value of crops increased from R$23 billion in 1996 to R$108 billion in 2006. In 2017, Brazilian agricultural output was worth approximately $168 bn. Brazil also has 170 million animals, which form the world's biggest commercial cattle herd.

AMAZON RAINFOREST

The Amazon rainforest has been utilised by Brazil and is a key part of the economy. Although the Amazon has generated a lot of wealth for Brazil its use by humans has created several problems.

The Amazon rainforest is spread over nine countries but Brazil has a 60% share of the rainforest and it takes up half of the country. The rainforest is home to thousands of different plants and animals as well as indigenous people. There are over 200 indigenous groups that speak over 120 languages.

WHAT IS IT USED FOR AND WHAT IS THE IMPACT?

Through a process of **deforestation** the Amazon rainforest has been cut down to make space for a range of money-making activities. Unfortunately, this deforestation has caused significant long-term problems.

Logging

The Amazon contains trees that can be cut down and sold for building supplies, furniture and charcoal. Hardwoods such as rosewood, mahogany and teak are in large demand from countries worldwide. For example, Japan imports 11 million cubic metres of wood every year.

Trees are also cut down to produce fuel that generates electricity for factories within the Amazon. For example, a steel factory requires millions of tons of wood for fuel each year.

The paper industry is also very significant in Brazil and one plant can produce pulp worth $5000 a day. But large areas of the rainforest have to be cut down to create space to grow pulpwood trees. Roads also have to be built to allow for transport in and out of the plants. For example, one plant in the Amazon has cut down 5600 square miles of rainforest to plant pulpwood trees and uses 2000 tons of wood to create electricity every day.

Grazing land

A large amount of the Amazon has been turned into grazing land for cattle ranches. In order to set up these ranches, trees and surrounding ecosystems have to be destroyed. Cattle ranches have rapidly increased in Brazil; production doubled between 1990 and 2002.

Using land for grazing has some devastating consequences:

- 80% of areas that have been torn down are used for grazing land.
- An area the size of Portugal was created for cattle ranching between 1996 and 2006.
- After the land has been used it is severely damaged and it will be years before anything can grow again.

Cattle ranch statistics
220 million cattle
20 million goats
60 million pigs
700 million chickens

Source of medicine

The Amazon rainforest is home to thousands of plants that are key components of life-saving drugs, but because of deforestation these plants and their homes are being destroyed.

- A quarter of medicines contain ingredients from the rainforest.
- 121 prescription drugs contain plants that can be located only in the rainforest.
- The US National Cancer Institute has discovered there are at least 3000 cancer-fighting plants in the world and 70% grow in the rainforest.

PROTECTING THE RAINFOREST

The Brazilian Government has put many policies in place to protect the rainforest.

Bolsa Floresta: Forest Conservation Allowance Programme

This programme was created in 2007 and aimed to reduce deforestation. After completing a 2-day training course and promising to carry out deforestation families were given a yearly benefit of R$1360. The programme also funded health and education projects in the local community. Sustainable businesses that did not require areas of rainforest to be cut down were also supported, such as fish farming and bee keeping.

Forest Code

This was set up in 1965 and is vital to the protection of the Amazon. The code protects certain areas, called legal reserves, and bans deforestation in certain high-risk areas such as slopes or rivers. More areas of the Amazon are being legally protected. For example, in 2006 a law protecting an area of 15 million hectares (the equivalent of Portugal, Denmark and Switzerland added together) in the state of Para was passed. This was great progress for the Amazon as this state is home to the country's largest timber production, most of which is carried out illegally, and a number of endangered species such as the giant anteater and the black spider monkey.

VIDEO LINK

Check out the clip 'Natural balance – threats to the rainforest' for more on this at www.brightredbooks.net/N5ModernStudies.

ONLINE

Check out the page 'Protecting the Brazilian Amazon' at www.brightredbooks.net/N5ModernStudies.

ONLINE TEST

Take the 'Inequalities in Brazil' test online at www.brightredbooks.net/N5ModernStudies.

THINGS TO DO AND THINK ABOUT

1 What are advantages and disadvantages of using the resources within the Amazon rainforest?

WORLD POWER: INDIA

BACKGROUND

As a result of trade influences in the region India was under British Raj (rule) from 1858 until 1947. India was able to gain its independence because of the work of a man called Mohandas 'Mahatma' Gandhi. Gandhi brought together Muslims and Hindus, and led a peaceful anti-British campaign, which involved techniques such as boycotting British goods and fasting. In 1947 the Indian Independence Act came into place, relinquishing British rule and dividing the area into two separate states: India and Pakistan.

FACT

India is also referred to as Bharat.

ONLINE

Research and create a fact file on Gandhi and his achievements.

FACT

India's electorate is bigger than the EU and USA electorates combined!

POLITICAL SYSTEM

India's political system is a **federal republic** and its structure is outlined in the Constitution, written in 1949. In a federal republic lots of smaller states have power but they are all overseen by one central government.

The Constitution is founded on the following principles:

- Justice
- Liberty
- Equality
- Fraternity

EXECUTIVE BRANCH

Within the executive branch there is a range of positions:

- President
- Vice-President
- Prime Minister
- Council of Ministers

President

The president serves for a 5-year term and leads the executive branch of India's government. It is his/her role to implement the laws passed by the legislative branch. The president is required to carry out the actions recommended to him/her by the government.

If parliament does not believe that the president is able to carry out this position the Lok Sabha can impeach him/her and the Rajya Sabha will investigate.

Powers:
- approve laws
- appoint a range of positions, including the prime minister and chief justice
- Commander-in-Chief of the armed forces
- pardoning powers.

The president is not elected by the people of India but rather by the members of an Electoral College. This Electoral College includes members of the parliament and legislative assemblies of the states and uses the single transferable vote system.

Government: prime minister and the Council of Ministers

The government is made up of the prime minister and the Council of Ministers.

It is the prime minister's job to appoint and head the Council of Ministers, and together they advise and support the president. Although the president appoints the prime minister he/she is normally the leader of the majority party in parliament.

DON'T FORGET

The president does not have unlimited power and must work with the other branches of government.

LEGISLATIVE BRANCH

The parliament, which consists of two houses, forms the law-making branch of government. The two houses of the Indian parliament are:

contd

- Council of State – Rajya Sabha
- House of the People – Lok Sabha.

Rajya Sabha

- Maximum 250 members.
- 238 from the 28 states and the 7 union territories.
- 12 nominated by the president and the rest elected by the people of India.
- 6-year term.
- Vice-president is the chairman.

Lok Sabha

- Maximum of 552 members.
- 530 from the states and 20 from the union territories.
- The president can nominate two from the Anglo-Indian community.
- 5-year term.
- All elected by the people of India.

The main role of the parliament is to make laws, and every new law has to be agreed on by both houses. The laws focus on issues that affect the whole of India, such as defence, currency, foreign affairs, customs and communications.

This system of government requires all branches to work together. For example the Lok Sabha will monitor the prime minister and the Council of Ministers, and if they doubt that they are fulfilling their role to the required standard a vote of confidence can be issued, causing the ministers to step down. The president's power is limited because if the Lok Sabha support the prime minister's decision the president cannot go against their action.

GENERAL ELECTIONS 2014

In 2014, 814.5 m people were eligible to vote in India's general election. This enormous electorate makes India the largest democracy in the world. There were 930,000 polling stations. The votes were counted using electronic voting machines. Over 8,000 candidates were in the running for only 543 seats. Because of the extensive size of the electorate, voting took place between 12 April and 7 May in ten stages.

On the 26 May 2014, Narendra Modi became the 14th Prime Minister of India. Modi belongs to the Bharatiya Janata Party and was elected to serve five years. Elections are due to take place in 2019.

The two main parties are the Indian National Congress and the Bharatiya Janata. However, it is very difficult for one party to gain enough seats to become a majority government and as a result several parties have formed coalitions under a number of names:

- United Progressive Alliance
- National Democracrtic Alliance
- Third Front
- Fourth Front.

JUDICIAL BRANCH

The most powerful court in India is called the Supreme Court and it is located in New Delhi.

The court deals with:
- disputes between government and state
- disputes between the states
- appeals from smaller courts.

There are 25 judges and one chief justice who are appointed by the president until they retire at the age of 65. They must ensure that the Constitution is upheld at all times.

STATES AND UNION TERRITORIES

India contains 28 states and 7 union territories. State government is structured in the same way as the national government. Each state has a governor who works with the chief minister and a Council of Ministers to deal with state issues.

FACT

Manmohan Singh was the second prime minster to ever be re-elected.

ONLINE

Head to the BrightRED Digital Zone to watch a detailed analysis of the 2014 General Election.

ONLINE TEST

Take the test on India's political system online at www.brightredbooks.net/N5ModernStudies.

ONLINE

For more about the Indian Government take a look at their website at www.brightredbooks.net/N5ModernStudies

THINGS TO DO AND THINK ABOUT

Make a diagram showing the different branches of the federal government in India.

INEQUALITIES IN INDIA: CASTE AND WEALTH

FACT

The population of India is bigger than those of the USA, Indonesia, Brazil and Pakistan combined!

VIDEO LINK

Check out the 'Caste system explained' clip to learn more at www.brightredbooks.net/N5ModernStudies.

DON'T FORGET

People who are victims of discrimination are often too scared to report it to the police.

ONLINE

Find out who the top 10 Indian billionaires are in 2018 at www.brightredbooks.net/N5ModernStudies.

VIDEO LINK

Check out the End Untouchability trailer at www.brightredbooks.net/N5ModernStudies.

POPULATION OF INDIA

India currently has almost 18% of the world's population, a staggering 1.34bn people, and will become the world's most populous country, overtaking China, by 2024.

HINDU CASTE SYSTEM

The Hindu caste system began nearly 3000 years ago when Indian society was separated into different types of work, also known as Varna. Over time this transformed into a rigid caste system. The caste a person belongs to is wholly dependent on birth and moving between the castes is not permitted.

There are four main castes:

- Brahmin
- Kshatriya
- Vaishya
- Shudra.

There is a final group of people who are not part of the caste system and are instead referred to as 'untouchables' or Dalits. This rigid system generated social tension and discrimination between the castes, in particular towards the untouchables. The Indian Constitution now states that caste discrimination is illegal and in 1989 the Scheduled Castes and Scheduled Tribes (Prevention of Atrocities) Act was passed by the government.

Although it is illegal to discriminate against a person based on caste, the Dalits frequently suffer violence and abuse. For example, children are forced to have lunch away from other students at school, and people are not allowed into certain temples, are refused service at shops and have been attacked for walking on certain streets. In 2005 one man's son and daughter-in-law were murdered as a result of them marrying between castes. The suspects were never charged and the case remains unresolved. Charities have reported that, in 2008, 33,000 crimes were recorded against Dalits, but the number is thought to be a lot higher as many crimes go unreported.

Dealing with the issue: Video Volunteers

Video Volunteers is an international organisation that seeks to use media as a tool to reveal poverty, injustice and inequality in India. Volunteers teach and support local people to gather evidence that is often not covered by the national media and campaign for the issue to be dealt with. In 2012 they launched the campaign 'Article 17' to put pressure on the government department responsible for dealing with protecting Dalits (the National Commission for Scheduled Castes). Through videos of Indians sharing their daily experiences of discrimination the group hope that the government will recognise the issue and take more steps to punish those who are responsible.

INDIA'S WEALTH

India's economy

Like Brazil, India is part of the BRICs nations and its economy has grown rapidly over the past 20 years. The Indian economy is expected to grow by approximately 8% per annum between 2018 and 2026. The number of wealthy people in India is also growing. For example, according to Forbes magazine, in 2012 there were 46 billionaires living in India; by 2018 this had increased to 119 billionaires.

contd

Wealth and income inequalities

Despite this progression there are vast wealth inequalities across the country. The distribution of India's wealth and success is not equal. The top 10% who earn the highest wages make almost 12 times more than the bottom 10%, which is the largest difference in all evolving economies.

Living in the slums

Across India there are 13.8 million households (64 million people) living in slums that have been classed as unsuitable. These homes often lack sanitation and electricity, and are very poorly built. For example a third of slum homes do not have an inside toilet and 64% do not have a working sewage system. Although slums can be found across the country some areas have more than others.

Percentages of households that live in slums:

- Kolkata: 30%
- Chennai: 29%
- New Delhi: 15%
- Bangalore: 9%

Profile: Mumbai

- Financial capital of India.
- Largest city, with a population of 19 million.
- 1 in 6 people lives in the slums.
- 40% of households live in shanty towns.

With regards to income levels India is becoming increasingly unequal. The ideal official measure of income inequality is 0, but over the last 25 years India's levels have increased from 0.32 to 0.5, its highest level since 1922. According to an investigation carried out by the Organisation for Economic Co-operation and Development (OECD) India has the highest number of poor people in the world, with 42% of the population surviving on less than $1.25 a day. Places such as Orissa, Chhattisgarh and Bihar in rural areas of central and eastern India are suffering the most.

Rural areas rely on farming to make a living, and 65% of the population are involved in agriculture. However, farmers often struggle to produce enough food to eat or sell, and live in poverty. A farming household will make, on average, 1800 Indian rupees a year.

Government support

Policy	Description
National Rural Employment Guarantee Act 2005	This policy gave all Indians living in rural areas the right to 100 days of paid work within 15 days of asking for it, and within 3 miles of their village
Public Distribution System	Shops have been set up to allocate funded food and other items to poor people across India

CASE STUDY: FARMERS IN BIHAR

Bihar is one the poorest states in India, with about 79% of the population living below the poverty line. Within Bihar farming is the main source of income; 75% of workers are employed in farming. State government, in partnership with the World Bank, has set up a project called the System of Crop Intensification. This project encourages farming methods that have been used across the world to improve farming output. The methods include seed treatment and planting without the use of chemical fertilisers or herbicides. Between 5 and 6 million farmers in China, Indonesia, Cambodia, Sri Lanka and Vietnam have increased their profits using this method. Around 103,000 farmers across the state have successfully followed the project, increasing their crop production and therefore their food supply and income. One farmer doubled his annual income to 100,000 rupees.

THINGS TO DO AND THINK ABOUT

1 Describe what daily life might be like for a Dalit.

2 What evidence is there to suggest that India is a wealthy country?

INEQUALITIES IN INDIA: WOMEN'S RIGHTS

WOMEN IN INDIA

Men and women are not equal within India. Women are viewed as the lesser sex and as a result have faced years of discrimination. They are seen as a burden to their families and their personal freedom is heavily restricted.

This preference for males has led to thousands of sex-selective abortions and a high number of child killings. Although these actions are illegal doctors are often bribed to tell the families the sex of a baby before it is born. Fewer and fewer girls are being born or surviving every year. The 2011 census discovered that India still prefers boys over girls, with the gap between boys and girls being high. In 2001 there were 927 girls for every 1000 boys under 6. By 2016 this widened to 898 for every 1000.

Life for women

A study carried out in 2012 by the Thomson Reuters Foundation revealed that out of the G20 countries India is the worst place for women to live. This is because of its high rates of infanticide, domestic slavery and child marriage.

Violence towards women is common and viewed as acceptable by many Indians. A study carried out by UNICEF discovered that 52% of teenage girls and 57% of boys believe that is acceptable for a husband to beat his wife. Crimes against women in everyday life have increased; between 2014 and 2016 sexual assault of women increased by 12–15% with other crimes against women rising by 3–5%.

Dowry payments

In the past when a woman got married her family paid a dowry to her husband and his family. This payment didn't always take the form of cash, it could be gifts such as cars or a new home. As a result of this system many women were abused. To deal with this issue the system was outlawed in the Dowry Prohibition Act (1961). This Act stated that giving or receiving any dowry exceeding 7000 rupees (£90) is illegal. Although the laws are commonly ignored, the police take dowry-related crimes seriously.

Domestic Violence Act 2005

The government passed an Act in 2005 that outlawed a range of domestic abuse against women. Under the Act physical, sexual and economic abuse are prohibited. Women also gained more rights under this Act. These rights include the right to continue living in a house even if she doesn't own it and the right to help and protection from police and health workers.

SUCCESSFUL WOMEN

Despite these challenges women across India are breaking with tradition and taking on important roles within society.

Naina Lal Kidwai

Naina is a very successful Indian businesswoman who has achieved a lot throughout her career. :
- she graduated from Harvard Business School.
- She is well-respected and was the former head of HSBC in India.
- She is currently the chair of the Indian Sanitation Coalition (to help clean up India).

Sonia Gandhi

Sonia Gandhi is a powerful and influential Indian politician. Born in Italy she married Rajiv Gandhi and moved to India. After her husband was assassinated she was

ONLINE TEST

Check out Sonia Gandhi's profile in Forbes magazine at www.brightredbooks.net/N5ModernStudies.

contd

reluctant to enter politics, but eventually joined the Indian National Congress in 1997. In 1998 she was elected president of the party and held the position until 2017. This makes her the longest-serving president of the Congress party in its 128 years. She has also held the position of chairperson of the ruling United Progressive Alliance in Lok Sabha since 2004.

CASE STUDY: DELHI

There are high levels of abuse and oppression of women in northern India, particularly in Delhi. For example, compared to cities of a similar size, Delhi has the highest recorded number of rape cases, with 1996 cases being reported in 2016. Delhi also has problems with murder and abduction, and in the same year it was deemed to be the most unsafe city in India, followed by Bengaluru and Mumbai according to the National Crime Records Bureau (NCRB). On average a rape case is reported every 18 hours and crimes of a sexual nature every 14. This issue received international attention after a brutal rape case in 2012.

The incident

A 23-year-old medical student was travelling on a bus in Delhi when she was beaten and raped by six men, including the bus driver. She was in hospital for 13 days before she died of her injuries.

The aftermath

While the young woman was in hospital, the people of India took to the streets demanding change and justice. Large protests were held the day after the rape happened. The police resorted to tear gas to stop protestors marching to the presidential palace.

'We are marching to create awareness among people that women should be respected. Because a woman is a mother, a woman is a sister, she is a wife and she is a daughter.' (National Commission for Women)

Despite their numbers, it took a week for the prime minister to address the case directly on TV. During a broadcast he asked for the protests to stop and made a pledge to make India a safer place.

Government response

Soon after the woman died it was decided that:
* police would patrol Delhi at night
* there would be checks on bus drivers
* buses with tinted windows would no longer be permitted
* information about convicted rapists would be made available to the public
* committees would be set up to investigate the problems.

Verdict:
* the four men guilty of carrying out the rape have been sentenced to death.

VIDEO LINK

Watch the BBC News report on protests following the incident at www.brightredbooks.net/ N5ModernStudies.

DON'T FORGET

Check the news for any new stories highlighting these issues and any progress that has been made.

ONLINE TEST

Take the test on 'Inequalities in India' online at www. brightredbooks.net/ N5ModernStudies.

THINGS TO DO AND THINK ABOUT

1   Create the front page of a newspaper for the day after the young student died. Consider the following points:
* what life is like for women in India
* what had happened to the woman
* how people reacted
* what changes the government wanted to put in place.

WORLD POWER: UNITED STATES OF AMERICA

JOURNEY THROUGH POLITICS

Like many countries, such as France and Australia, America's political system is outlined in its Constitution. The American Constitution was created in 1787 with the purpose of explaining the different branches of government and the powers they had been granted. It was important that power was not held by just one branch; this is why the powers are separated and divided. All of the branches have to work together under a system of checks and balances. The Constitution can be, and has been, amended. The first set of changes that were made is referred to as the Bill of Rights.

BRANCHES OF AMERICAN GOVERNMENT

The federal government has the power to deal with issues that have an impact on all American states. These issues include:

- currency
- disputes between states
- armed forces
- postal services
- defence
- foreign affairs.

Although there is one government in charge of the whole of America, each of the 50 states has its own government with power over local issues such as:

- education
- punishments
- local taxes
- road provisions.

Both federal and state governments contain three branches: executive, judicial and legislative.

REPRESENTATION IN AMERICAN POLITICS

The executive

The president heads the executive branch of the federal government. He or she must be an American-born citizen and at least 35 years of age. Presidents can only serve two terms of 4 years in office. The powers of the president are outlined in Article 2 of the Constitution.

Chief legislator	Chief diplomat	Chief executive	Commander-in-chief
• Makes recommendations to Congress • Vetoes Bills	• Creates foreign policy and treaties • Represents the USA in foreign relations	• Appoints officials • Supervises the administration of executive department • Ensures laws are followed	• Decides on war strategies during war • Deploys the military in times of disorder

The legislative

The legislative branch is made up of Congress, which contains the Senate and House of Representatives. American citizens can vote for people to represent them in both Houses. The Senate is made up of two representatives from each state, who serve for up to 6 years. In the House of Representatives each state has roughly one representative for every 400,000 citizens, which results in 435 altogether. Together, these two Houses create America's laws.

Supreme Court

American citizens do not vote for the judges of the Supreme Court. Instead, the president nominates judges and they are approved or rejected by Congress. Supreme Court judges represent American citizens as it is their job to ensure that no laws conflict with the Constitution or American citizens' rights.

GETTING INVOLVED

America is a democratic country and therefore political involvement from citizens is crucial. There are many ways in which American people can participate in the political system and voice their views and opinions.

Join a political party

The two main political parties in America are the Democrat Party and the Republican Party. If citizens join a political party, there are many different ways they can contribute:

- during state primaries they can vote for who they think should be the party's candidate for president
- attend party campaign rallies
- hand out leaflets, stickers and badges promoting their party's candidates
- telephone voters to persuade them to vote for their candidate.

Standing as a candidate/voting

To ensure that all branches of government correctly reflect the views of the population, Americans have the right to vote. If they believe they would be successful at representing the public's views they can stand as a candidate themselves. For example:

- local level: mayor
- state level: governor
- federal level: president

Citizens can also vote on specific issues known as Ballot Measures of Propositions, e.g.:

- Californian 2018 Three States Initiative
- Utah 2018 Medical Marijuana Initiative

Interest groups

Interest groups try to use their influence to persuade the public to put pressure on politicians either to change or not to change the law. If citizens feel strongly about an issue, they can share their views through a group.

DONALD TRUMP

Donald J. Trump is the 45th President of the United States of America and has courted controversy since assuming office in January 2017. Trump won the election over Hillary Clinton with 306 Electoral College Votes. Trump has divided both America and the international community and, since his election victory, has never been far from the media spotlight. Here are some of his domestic and foreign policies.

Domestic policies	Foreign policy
Defend the right to keep and bear arms (second amendment of US constitution)	Challenge China's export subsidies, IP theft and Cyber attacks
Tackle Gang Culture (and drug abuse)	Increase the size and strength of US army
Create Energy Independence	Tackle Radical Islam
Boost the American Steel Industry	Support middle-eastern allies in bringing down ISIS
Tackle fraudulent welfare claims	Denuclearisation of North Korea

2016 presidential election

Once again in 2016, as was the case in 2012, social media sites such as Twitter and Facebook had an influential role. However, on this occasion, one of the main areas of controversy was the Russian state's alleged involvement in attempting to influence the American electorate by using social media platforms to circulate false content.

Trump won the election with the majority of support coming from men (53%). He had a particularly low support from black voters (8%) and Hispanic voters (29%). White voters made up 70% of the voters.

THINGS TO DO AND THINK ABOUT

Make a table comparing the ways American and British citizens can participate in their country's political systems.

DON'T FORGET

It is really important that you have real-life American examples to support your points.

DON'T FORGET

Remember, the American system does not have MPs or MSPs!

ONLINE

Research the ethos behind the three American interest groups illustrated at www.brightredbooks.net/N5ModernStudies.

ONLINE

Visit www.brightredbooks.net/N5ModernStudies for more statistics from the 2016 election.

ONLINE TEST

Test your knowledge of American politics online at www.brightredbooks.net/N5ModernStudies.

UNITED STATES OF AMERICA: IMMIGRATION

IMMIGRATION

The USA is a country founded on immigrants; for years people have travelled from all over the world to pursue the American dream. Ellis Island in New York opened in 1892 and saw 12 million immigrants pass through its doors into America.

Population breakdown

The USA's population is made up of a range of ethnic groups.

Ethnic group	Percentage of population
White	72.4
Hispanic	16.3
Black	12.6
Asian and Pacific Islander	4.8
Native American	0.9

Figures for 2010.

According to information gathered from the 2010–2011 census there are over 50 million legal and illegal immigrants currently living in the USA. Between 2000 and 2010, immigration increased the population by 22.5 million, which is 80% of the total population growth.

ARGUMENTS IN FAVOUR OF IMMIGRATION

History

Immigration is a huge part of American history and millions of immigrants have contributed to the success of the country. Many people argue that it would be unfair to shut the doors when so many immigrants have enriched America.

Culture

The American population is often referred to as a 'melting pot'. This is the idea that many different races and traditions have joined together to form the American population. This mix means that America has a diverse and varied culture, and is an interesting place to live.

Economy

There is a common stereotype that immigrants take jobs from American citizens or do not contribute to the economy in any way, but this is not true. Many immigrants fill job shortages in America, particularly in the Southern states, and are willing to do low-skilled and low-paid jobs that American citizens do not want to do.

ARGUMENTS AGAINST IMMIGRATION

Social problems

Immigrants can decide not to embrace American culture or tradition, but rather create their own separate areas in towns and cities. For example, 78% of immigrant school children speak English as a second language. As immigrants are willing to work for lower amounts of money this drives down wages and makes it harder for USA citizens to find well-paid jobs, which can also create tensions.

contd

Crime

Many people are smuggled into America, therefore are living there illegally. Some citizens think this is unfair because they are getting the benefits of living in the country without contributing in ways such as paying tax. Illegal immigrants are also more likely to be involved in organised crimes such as drug dealing.

Cost to taxpayers

Immigrants are much more likely to receive welfare and be supported by the government as the table below indicates. This angers some citizens as they feel their tax money is being spent supporting immigrants.

Welfare Use 2012

	US born	Foreign born
Medicaid	23%	42%
Food	22%	40%
Cash Welfare	10%	12%
Housing	6%	6%

(Survey of Income and Programme Participation, 2012 data)

ONLINE

To find out more about America's Immigration laws have changed over time, visit the Digital Zone at www.brightredbooks.net/N5ModernStudies.

BARACK OBAMA

Obama's immigration policy had four key aims.

Aim	Description	Progress
Increase border control	Reduce the number of people illegally crossing the border into America	The number of people patrolling the border doubled from 10,000 in 2004 to 21,000 in 2011. For the first time the south-west border, between California and Texas, has aerial surveillance
Monitor businesses	Ensure companies only employ legal immigrants	From 2009 the number of companies involved in e-verification has doubled and is now 416,000
Improve the citizenship system	Make it possible for illegal immigrants to gain citizenship	A way of streamlining the system is being developed
Streamline the system	Make it simpler for people to work and study in America	The time families have to spend apart has been reduced

DONALD TRUMP ON IMMIGRATION

- In his short time in office, Trump has opted to go a totally different route from Obama.
- In 2017, he banned refugees from entering the USA for a four-month period.
- In 2017, he introduced a travel ban on eight countries – Chad, Iran, Libya, North Korea, Somalia, Syria, Venezuela and Yemen.
- In 2018, he replaced Obama's Deferred Action for Childhood Arrivals (DACA) Programme with a new Immigration Plan which, amongst other things, budgets for a $25 billion wall along the Mexican border.

VIDEO LINK

Hear Donald Trump's controversial views on Immigration on the Digital Zone.

IMMIGRATION AND PROTESTS

Many believe Donald Trump's immigration policies to be unjust and an attack on the poorest people in the USA. In May 2018, protestors took to the streets of New York to vent their anger at Trump's decision to bring to an end the temporary protected status which was introduced to protect immigrants from countries affected by conflict or natural disasters. In 2017, following Trump's decision to remove DACA, students in Colorado staged a school walk-out to highlight their disgust at ending a programme that saved 0.8m immigrants from deportation.

FACT

During April and May 2018, 1,995 children were removed from the care of their parents when they were caught trying to illegally cross the US-Mexico border. Furthermore, the adults will be now be prosecuted. Illegally crossing the border for the first time was previously, during the time of President Obama, classed a minor offence (BBC News, June 2018).

THINGS TO DO AND THINK ABOUT

1. Why might a person want to leave a country and choose to live in America?
2. Create a poster that highlights the conflicting approaches of Obama and Trump in attempting to deal with America's immigration problems.

UNITED STATES OF AMERICA: INEQUALITIES

In this section we are going to investigate whether or not every American has the same chances to succeed.

DON'T FORGET

Asian and Pacific Islanders have the best health and do very well in school.

FACT

Black men are five times more likely to die of HIV/Aids than white men.

FACT

A 2017 report published by the US Centers for Disease Control and Prevention found that in 2015 infant mortality rates were higher for blacks (11.7% per 1,000 live births) than for whites (4.8% per 1,000 live births).

DON'T FORGET

Many Hispanic people are in the USA illegally and therefore are not able to access health care.

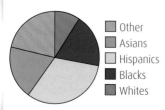

- Other
- Asians
- Hispanics
- Blacks
- Whites

Percentage of people without health insurance.

ONLINE

Check out the breakdown of the US healthcare system at www.brightredbooks.net/N5ModernStudies.

HEALTH

Country	Life expectancy	Infant mortality per 1000 live births
USA	80 years	5.8
UK	80.8 years	4.3
France	82.9 years	3.2
Singapore	85.2 years	2.4

CIA World Factbook 2017

Health inequalities can be split into two areas:
- level of health
- access to health care.

LEVEL OF HEALTH

Minorities suffer poorer health than whites, particularly the black population. From birth, blacks and Hispanics are more likely to suffer poor health. They have higher rates of obesity, heart disease and HIV/AIDS. These groups are also more likely to have a substance abuse problem. Whites will attend check-ups and health screenings, and therefore are able to identify any health problems early on. This is not the case with blacks and Hispanics. Having poorer health has a life-long impact, leading to further problems later in life.

ACCESS TO HEALTH CARE

Within the USA health care is not funded by the government, instead it is a private system and citizens have to pay for it themselves. They do this through health insurance, which they fund themselves or have provided as part of their job. However, an estimated 11/3% of US adults do not have health insurance, with minority groups having the highest percentage of people without health insurance.

Even when citizens have health insurance they are often denied treatment or given a limit to the amount of treatment they are allowed to receive.

There are government benefits available: Medicaid and Medicare. Medicaid is for people who have a low income or have additional needs, such as a disability. Medicare is for people 65 years old and over. Although these benefits are available, they don't always cover the treatments required, hospitals are understaffed and don't always have the same access to resources or technology.

Affordable Care Act

This Act has been nicknamed 'Obamacare' and is a range of health reforms that were signed by Obama in 2010. The Act:

- prevents children with pre-existing health problems being rejected by health insurance companies
- removes lifetime treatment caps
- funds small businesses to allow them to be able to provide health care to their workers
- increases free preventive care, for example cancer screenings
- discounts a range of prescription drugs used via Medicare.
- Trump has stated he wants to abolish Obamacare, however, he is a long way from doing so
- Many American businesses are annoyed by Trump's insistence that they should offer health insurance or be financially penalised (ironically, this was a feature of Obamacare).

EDUCATION

Dropout rates

Ethnic group	Percentage 0f 18-24 year-olds dropping out of high school
Asian and Pacific Islander	4
White	5
Black	8
Hispanic	14

(US Census Bureau, 2015)

Postcode lottery

There are extensive differences between schools in suburbs and schools located in inner city ghetto areas. Suburban schools are better funded and as a result provide a higher quality of education compared to poorly funded ghetto schools.

Suburban school

- New technology.
- Highly qualified teachers who enjoy teaching there.
- Many sports and extracurricular opportunities.
- Education is highly valued.

Ghetto school

- Run down and old buildings.
- Drug and alcohol issues.
- Limited resources, i.e. textbooks or computers.
- Teachers who don't want to teach there.
- Focus is on a future with gangs rather than further education.

Language barrier

One in four school children in the USA speak English as a second language. For students with very limited English school can be very challenging and they often feel isolated. They may struggle to understand teachers or make friends.

Role models

In ghettos and barrios there is a lack of positive role models to inspire young people. Rather than hoping to move on to further education and have a successful job, young people in ghettos and barrios want to grow up and be part of local gangs.

VIDEO LINK

Learn more about the American education system by watching the clip at www.brightredbooks.net/N5ModernStudies.

FACT

60% of black people in the USA that have dropped out of school have served time in prison.

FACT

75% of crimes are committed by high-school dropouts.

FACT

90% of jobs in USA require a high-school education.

ONLINE TEST

Test your knowledge of inequalities in the USA online at www.brightredbooks.net/N5ModernStudies.

AFFIRMATIVE ACTION

Some universities have specific race targets and goals to meet and as a result make it easier for minority groups to gain a place over white or Asian candidates. In the past Affirmative Action programmes had a positive impact and appeared to be reducing the education gap. For example, in 1960 5.4% of black people aged 25–29 graduated from college, this had increased to 15.4% in 1995. According to the Economic Policy Institute (EPI) black high school graduations have increased from 54% in 1968 to 92% in 2018.

However, in current times many white and Asian students feel that they are being subjected to discrimination when a less-able minority student gains a place instead of them. Groups have campaigned against Affirmative Action programmes and many individuals have taken their cases to court. For example, the University of Michigan had an Affirmative Action scheme that allocated extra admission points to minority groups to boost their chances of meeting the required score. However, in 2003 the Supreme Court declared the scheme to be unconstitutional.

THINGS TO DO AND THINK ABOUT

1. When considering health statistics in the USA, the UK, Singapore and France, where would you prefer to live? Give two reasons to support your decision.
2. What challenges do children in the ghetto face when trying to gain an education?
3. Do you think Affirmative Action programmes are a good idea? Give at least three reasons for your answer.

HUMAN RIGHTS

VIDEO LINK

Head to the BrightRED Digital Zone to find out what it is like to live in Syria under the regime at Basher-el-Assad.

VIDEO LINK

Check out the video to find out about human rights violations against women in Syria at www.brightredbooks. net/N5ModernStudies.

United Nations

FACT

The Universal Declaration of Human Rights sets the Guinness World Record for Most Translated Document. It has been translated into 403 different languages.

ONLINE

Using the UN website research different human rights bodies and their specific roles.

DON'T FORGET

Countries have different rights enshrined in law, therefore not every country has the same rights. For example, owning a gun in America is a right protected by law, but this is not the case in the UK.

HUMAN RIGHTS VIOLATIONS IN SYRIA

Bashar al-Assad became President of Syria in 2000. In 2010, a sequence of revolutions, referred to as the Arab Spring, saw the governments of Tunisia and Egypt being overthrown by their people. This inspired the population of Syria to rise against Bashar al-Assad. Many Syrians believed that al-Assad was a corrupt dictator. In 2011, protesters campaigned for al-Assad's resignation, but the President refused to tolerate what he deemed to be 'foreign-backed terrorism' and unleashed the might of the Syrian army on his people. Over the past seven years, a full-scale civil war has erupted with ongoing human rights violations. As of March 2018:

- The death toll is estimated at 353,900 (including over 100,000 civilians).
- 56,900 people are still missing, presumed to be dead.
- 847 medical personnel killed (and almost 500 attacks on medical facilities).
- Multiple shootings, shelling and air strikes.
- 53% of Syrians have been displaced.
- Alleged chemical attacks on innocent civilians (this is disputed by al-Assad).

(BBC News, March 2018)

THE UNITED NATIONS

Set up in 1945 with just 51 members; the UN is an international organisation dedicated to promoting security, social progress and human rights throughout the world. The founding member states created a document known as the Declaration of Human Rights. This document is very important as it outlines and protects the rights of people across the world. Human rights have been enshrined in international law and the member states have made a commitment to develop them within their countries. The UN protects these human rights and can intervene when people are being denied them.

The Office of the High Commissioner for Human Rights is in charge of supporting the UN's Human Rights network. This network is divided into charter-based bodies and treaty-based bodies.

The Human Rights Council is a charter-based body that researches, reports and monitors human rights in countries and specific events of human rights violations. The Council works with the Office of the High Commissioner for Human Rights. The Council meets for 10 weeks a year and has 47 elected UN member states that serve 3-year terms. However, in June 2018, US Ambassador to the UN Nikki Haley announced that America would be leaving the UNHRC referring to it as a 'cesspool of political bias'. America is concerned by some of the organisation's members, many of whom have extremely poor human rights records.

contd

UN SECURITY COUNCIL

China, France, Russia, the United Kingdom and the United States of America are permanent members of the UN Security Council and have the power to prevent resolutions going through. This is known as a veto. It is not unusual for Russia to use its veto in relation to decisions concerning Syria. One example from February 2017 was when China and Russia blocked a draft resolution to place sanctions on those involved in producing or using chemical weapons in Syria. Another, in April 2017, when Russia vetoed a draft resolution which called for an investigation into a gas attack which took place on Khan Sheikhoun in Idlib province.

SUPPORTING SYRIA

There are a range of UN specialised agencies, funds and programmes operating in Syria and surrounding countries which aim to support the Syrian people in their time of need. The following table highlights some of this support.

United Nations Children's Fund (UNICEF)	• Helping provide life-saving supplies including clothes, food, clean water, medical care, education and protection • Providing Child Friendly Spaces for vulnerable children, which offer learning and psychological care as well as a safe place to rest and play
World Health Organisation (WHO)	• Providing humanitarian health assistance • Providing medical equipment and ambulances • Vaccinating children against childhood diseases
United Nations High Commission For Refugees (UNHCR)	• Providing Syrian refugees with cash for food, medicine and clothing • Appealing for donations to help fund new projects • Providing protection services and psychosocial support
World Food Programme (WFP)	• Supporting vulnerable groups, such as children under five years old and pregnant women, ensuring they remain nourished • Running a snack programme in over 400 schools • Providing support in generating income through sustainable farming
United Nations Development Programme (UNDP)	• Running local development programmes • Provided assistance to 4,647,000 Syrians • Provided almost 90,000 monthly jobs to those who have been displaced

THINGS TO DO AND THINK ABOUT

Look at the table above. What specific rights are these agencies protecting and promoting in other countries?

DON'T FORGET

Always try and link the work carried out by the UN to the needs of the country.

FACT

Many Syrian refugees who have been forced to flee their homeland have found themselves in countries like Iraq and Turkey.

VIDEO LINK

For more on the Arab Spring, watch the clip at www.brightredbooks.net/N5ModernStudies.

ONLINE

For a CNN comprehensive timeline of the events which have taken place in Syria between 2011–18, please visit www.brightredbooks.net/N5ModernStudies.

'Syria is the biggest humanitarian and refugee crisis of our time, a continuing cause of suffering for millions which should be garnering a groundswell of support around the world.'

Filippo Grandi, UNHCR High Commissioner

FACT

Almost 50% of Syrian refugees were children.

ONLINE TEST

Check how much you have learned about human rights in Syria and the UN online at www.brightredbooks.net/N5ModernStudies.

HUMAN RIGHTS AND INTERNATIONAL PRESSURE GROUPS

As we have learned from the previous section, human rights are promoted and protected by international alliances such as the UN. However, other organisations also support the development of human rights across the world. These organisations take the form of pressure groups and have members from different countries coming together to take action to prevent human rights abuses. They can form to address local, national or international issues. In this section we are going to look at the role the international pressure group Amnesty International has had in protecting human rights since its founding in 1961.

ONLINE

For more about what Amnesty International does check out its website at www.brightredbooks.net/N5ModernStudies.

VIDEO LINK

Check out the Amnesty International videos page at www.brightredbooks.net/N5ModernStudies to learn more.

AMNESTY INTERNATIONAL

'We are a campaigning organisation; it's what we do. Our purpose is to protect people wherever justice, fairness, freedom and truth are denied.' Amnesty International website.

The notion that ordinary people can influence the world and as a result make a tremendous difference is the founding principle of Amnesty International. When the group was originally formed the focus was on helping people who had been unfairly imprisoned. Over the years it has contributed to the release of thousands of prisoners all over the world. Since its creation the group has expanded its area of work and campaigned against a wider range of human rights abuses, for example cases of torture, unexplained disappearances, political killings, the death penalty and gay rights abuses. Amnesty International is an independent organisation that is not controlled, influenced or financed by any government. By 2005 it had become the largest independent human rights group in the world, with 1.8 million members. It has continued to grow and in 2018 membership and support are estimated to be approximately 7 m.

In order to defend human rights Amnesty International has two main strategies:
1   Develop awareness through education projects based on the principles of the UN Declaration of Human Rights.
2   Conduct research and challenge specific cases of human rights abuses across the world.

CAMPAIGNS

Amnesty International has several campaigns running at the same time. However, one of its long-standing focuses has been to abolish the death penalty in every country in the world. It believes that using this form of punishment breaks the right to life and the right not be tortured or subjected to cruel, inhuman or degrading punishment.

Rank	Country	Number of Executions
1	Iran	507
2	Saudi Arabia	146
3	Iraq	125
4	Pakistan	60
5	Egypt	35

Figures from Amnesty International, 2018.

Despite Amnesty International's campaign the use of the death penalty does not break international law nor is it seen to breach human rights when carried out correctly. Amnesty International has discovered that the number of countries that have the death penalty and the number that actually use it is declining. In 2018, 57 countries still have the death penalty as a punishment. Discrimination and incorrect sentencing are common in death penalty cases and it is therefore not always used correctly.

contd

Stance on death penalty	Number of countries	Example countries
Without death penalty	141	Denmark, Cambodia, Spain, Poland
With death penalty	57	USA, Sudan, China, Cuba

THE DEATH PENALTY AND CHILDREN

It is illegal to execute children and doing so breaks international law. Amnesty International campaigns to help to combat this abuse of human rights. Amnesty International has recorded 9 cases of child execution since 2016. All of these executions were carried out in Iran.

Case studies

Name	Country	Year of conviction	Age at conviction	Crime
Amirhossein Poursafar	Iran	2018	16	Rape and murder of a three-year-old girl
Ali Kazemi	Iran	2018	15	Alleged murder
Mahboubeh Mofidi	Iran	2018	17	Murder of husband

Crimes such as murder, terrorism, rape, drug trafficking, adultery and treason are punishable by death in both Iran and Sudan. Although the Sudan Child Act of 2010 states that no child under 18 can be executed, there is often controversy when determining the individual's real age. Despite international law it has been reported that Iran has more than 160 individuals under 18 on death row. Government officials state that they still abide by international law as they do not carry out executions until prisoners have turned 18.

AMNESTY INTERNATIONAL'S WORK

There are different actions that Amnesty International will take to prevent the use of the death penalty for both children and adults.

- Petition for the release of individual prisoners.

- Carry out research to create reports. These reports allow trends and individual cases to be identified and shared with the international community.

- Work with other human rights pressure groups such as the World Coalition Against the Death Penalty. This organisation brings together over 70 pressure groups, with Amnesty International being the founding member.

- Work with the UN to prohibit use of the death penalty.

THINGS TO DO AND THINK ABOUT

1 Would you consider joining a human rights pressure group? Give at least three reasons to explain your answer.

2 What forms of punishment do young offenders receive in Scotland?

3 Debate: Do you think the death penalty should be used as a form of punishment? Do you think it should be used on children and adults?

4 Using the Amnesty International website, try to find out about the different campaigns that it is currently running.

FACT

In May 2005 the US Supreme Court ruled that carrying out executions on children was unconstitutional and they prohibited it from happening. All world states also agreed that it should be made illegal.

FACT

It wasn't until 1998 that the UK parliament voted to completely abolish the death penalty. Up until then it could still be used as a punishment for treason or piracy. This change was a result of pressure from Amnesty International.

FACT

China still actively uses the death penalty, but refuses to release figures on capital punishment. It is estimated that China executes more people than the rest of the world combined, thought to be thousands.

FACT

In 2017, 23 countries carried out executions.

DON'T FORGET

The correct use of the death penalty does not break international law, but Amnesty International aims to abolish it in every country across the world.

DON'T FORGET

Remember, you have already learned about the role of pressure groups in democracy on pages 36 and 37.

DON'T FORGET

There are other international pressure groups that campaign against the death penalty, for example Human Rights Watch.

ONLINE TEST

Check how much you have learned about human rights and international pressure groups online at www.brightredbooks.net/N5ModernStudies.

HUMAN RIGHTS AND LOCAL RESPONSES

RECAP

So far this chapter has highlighted some of the human rights problems that exist across the world and the groups that try and address those problems. We have covered the work of the UN and the international charity organisation Amnesty International. This final section will explain the ways in which local people have taken action to improve their own human rights. We will be looking at two case studies:

1   women's rights in Afghanistan

2   Pussy Riot's fight in Russia

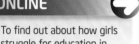

ONLINE

To find out about how girls struggle for education in Afghanistan, please visit www.brightredbooks.net/N5ModernStudies.

AFGHANISTAN: THE SITUATION

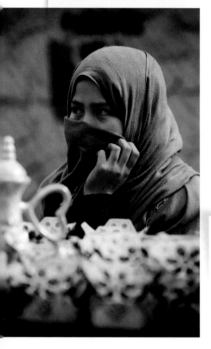

The Taliban are an extreme Islamist organisation that gained control of a large part of Afghanistan in 1994. When they were in power they enforced strict Islamic law, and women and girls were denied a wide range of rights. During their rule they were denied an education, employment and health care, and had to be accompanied by a man wherever they went. After the invasion of Afghanistan, led by the USA, in 2001 the Tailban were removed from power and the rights of women have gradually improved. They are now permitted to work again, with many becoming politicians, lawyers and doctors. The new constitution implemented in 2004 states 'the citizens of Afghanistan – whether man or woman – have equal rights and duties before the law'. Despite this, many women in rural areas are heavily controlled by their families and denied human rights. Although there have been changes in the law, changes in attitudes have been more difficult to achieve, for example women are forced into unwanted marriages and schools with female students have been burned down. In 2018, 85% of Afghanistan's 3.5m children who don't attend school are girls and Afghanistan's government provides significantly more schools for boys than it does for girls. This is true at both primary and secondary level.

LOCAL ACTION

March 2018 protest

When a car bomb killed 14 people and wounded another 47 in March 2018, protesters gathered in Lashkar Gah to campaign for an end to the war. The group was made up of members of the general public who threatened to march to a Taliban stronghold elsewhere in the Helmand province.

Afghanaid

This is a charity organisation that focuses solely on Afghanistan. One of its aims is to improve the position of women in their local areas. Many women have successfully taken advantage of the support offered by this local charity and as a result have acted as positive role models for other Afghan women. For example, an 18-year-old woman named Shahnaz Jan took part in a business project offered by Afghanaid. She now runs her own cosmetics shop, allowing her to earn her own income. Her story is an inspiration for young women, who hopefully will follow in her footsteps.

Revolutionary Association of the Women of Afghanistan

The Revolutionary Association of the Women of Afghanistan (RAWA) was set up in 1977 to improve peace, freedom, democracy and rights for women within Afghanistan. Its priority is to help women who have been affected by war and denied their human rights by other groups. They have educational, financial and health care projects, for example they have mobile health teams in eight provinces. These groups provide free care for those who cannot afford it and hold free first-aid courses for local women.

PUSSY RIOT: THE SITUATION

Pussy Riot are an all-girl punk band from Russia who are known for their bright balaclavas and controversial lyrics. The band sing songs that voice opinions against Russia's president, Vladimir Putin, and the system of government in Russia. After they carried out a flashmob in an Orthodox cathedral in Moscow on 21 February 2012, the band were arrested and eventually received a 2-year jail sentence. The band were charged with hooliganism and racial hatred, and it was believed that they were a threat to the public. One member, Yekaterina Samutsevich, was released after an appeal, but the remaining band members are still in prison.

However, this is no simple case; the band members generated great controversy throughout Russia and many other countries around the world. Pro Pussy Riot supporters believe that the girls are being punished for speaking out against the president rather than generating religious hatred. They believe that the punishment they received was too harsh and highlighted the lack of the political freedom of speech in Russia. The international community shares similar views, with America, the UK and the EU stating that the punishment was 'disproportionate'.

ACTION

Methods:
- protests
- fundraisers
- petitions
- letter writing
- celebrity support.

Soon after the girls were placed in custody protests erupted in Russia, with over 15,000 people campaigning for their release. Many people recognised that the act was disrespectful but believed the punishment went against their human rights. Letters were sent by the head of the church requesting the case be dropped and groups opposing Putin claim the stunt was 'idiotic but not dangerous'.

The campaign grew even stronger when it was revealed that the members were facing a possible 7-year jail sentence for their crimes. This attracted international attention, with protests being held in Paris, Kiev, Belgrade, Berlin, London, Dublin and Barcelona. Within Russia over 25,000 citizens requesting their release and artists' freedom of speech signed a petition. The public also showed their support during the trial as hundreds of people gathered outside the courtroom.

After being released from prison in 2013, Nadya Tolokonnikova and Maria Alyokhina set up a non-governmental organisation (NGO) called Zona Prava which aims to improve conditions for Russian prisoners. According to their website, 'Zona Prava unites people who want to see changes in Russia's prison system'.

THINGS TO DO AND THINK ABOUT

1 Imagine you are a journalist who has been sent to report on what life is like for women under Taliban rule. Write a story explaining what you discover.

2 Describe, in detail, the different methods that Pussy Riot campaigners used to fight for their freedom.

3 Can you think of any other ways that local people could support campaigns like these?

VIDEO LINK
Check out the clip of Pussy Riot getting attacked by Police with whips in Sochi in 2012 at www.brightredbooks.net/N5ModernStudies.

FACT
In February 2018, two members of Pussy Riot went 'missing' in Crimea. They were later found safe and well.

FACT
Madonna and Franz Ferdinand campaigned for Pussy Riot during their concerts in Moscow.

ONLINE TEST
Check how much you have learned about human rights and local response online at www.brightredbooks.net/N5ModernStudies.

DON'T FORGET
There are also groups that have been set up to fight against these campaigns.

CHILD SOLDIERS

WHAT IS A CHILD SOLDIER?

The international community has decided that a child soldier is any person under the age of 18 that is involved in an armed force or group. It doesn't matter if they are part of a rebel or government-supported organisation. Child soldiers can fulfil a range of roles, not just that of a fighter, for example cook, spy, porter, messenger or sex slave. In 2018, Child Soldiers International created the Child Soldiers World Index which highlighted that since 2016 children have been used in conflict in at least 18 countries. Worldwide, it is estimated that there are approximately 300,000 child soldiers, many of whom are under the age of 12. The number of child soldiers is difficult to record as the number frequently changes and countries are reluctant to tell the truth.

VIDEO LINK

Find out why child soldiers are used in the Democratic Republic of Congo at www.brightredbooks.net/N5ModernStudies.

WHY SHOULD WE LEARN ABOUT CHILD SOLDIERS?

Despite national and international laws that control the age at which individuals can fight and the age at which they can lawfully be recruited, many countries still permit the use of child soldiers. Countries either recruit and use child soldiers in their forces and organisations or can do nothing to stop rebel groups using them.

These types of actions go against treaties, laws and promises that countries have made and they deny children their fundamental rights. Life as a child soldier is extremely difficult and can result in long-term physical and psychological problems.

Democratic Republic of Congo (DRC)	In 2017, more than 3,000 child soldiers were recruited to play a role in the South Sundanese Conflict
Myanmar	Children aged 11 have been forced to join the national army
Colombia	Rebel groups have been found to use thousands of children during conflicts
India	Children aged 6 have been kidnapped and forced to join armed groups
Yemen	In 2017, according to UN figures, 1,700 children were recruited to fight in Yemen, which is suffering from severe famine.

ONLINE

Check out the Human Rights Watch website at www.brightredbooks.net/N5ModernStudies.

LAWS

A range of national and international agreements have been made in order to prevent and protect child soldiers across the world.

Convention on the Rights of the Child (1989)

After being agreed on by the UN General Assembly in 1989 this Convention came into place in 1990. Currently all UN member states have signed and ratified the Convention apart from Somalia and the USA.

The Convention includes 45 Articles outlining the rights of the child. Article 1 clarifies that a child is any person under the age 18. The Convention prevents anyone under the age of 15 being recruited or used in armed conflicts.

Optional Protocol to the Convention on the Rights of the Child on the Involvement of Children in Armed Conflict (2000)

FACT

The Convention on the Rights of the Child came into being in the UK in 1992, after it was signed in 1990.

In 2000 there were two Optional Protocols added to the Convention. The first required the minimum age of individuals directly involved in armed conflicts and compulsory recruitment to be raised to 18. The second protocol prohibited the sexual exploitation and abuse of children. These changes were the result of the international community's continued commitment to protecting children.

contd

International criminal law (1998)

The International Criminal Court deals with war crimes, crimes against humanity and genocide. Under the Rome Statute (1998), the recruitment and use of children under the age of 15 is a war crime. This applies to both government and non-government groups.

International labour law

In 1973 the International Labour Organisation required countries to abolish child labour and set the age limit for work that may impact on health and safety at 18. In 1999 this was developed further with the Worst Forms of Child Labour Convention. This Convention outlined participation in armed conflicts as the worst form of child labour and therefore it should not be a role for anyone under the age of 18.

International humanitarian law (1977)

Four international treaties were created in 1949 to control and decrease the effects of armed conflicts. These treaties are referred to as the Geneva Convention and their priority is to protect those who are not partaking in the conflict. A protocol added in 1977 declared 15 to be the age at which individuals can be recruited and used in conflicts.

African Charter on the Rights and Welfare of the Child (1999)

This is the only regional charter in the world to include sections regarding child soldiers. The charter states that no-one under the age of 18 is permitted to be directly involved in armed conflicts.

PROBLEMS WITH THE LAWS

Louder Than Words (2012), a report carried out by Child Soldiers International, discovered that despite these wide-ranging international laws and treaties countries are still failing to protect children from becoming child soldiers.

The table below outlines the main problems with the laws regarding child soldiers.

Point	Explain	Example
Some countries still permit the use of children for war in certain circumstances.	Although the country has agreed to the specification in treaties and international law it has adapted them slightly.	Vietnam law states that no child shall be used in armed conflict unless there is a significant threat to national independence.
Children in military schools can be involved in conflict situations.	In these cases the government require more personnel and have defended their actions by claiming that the personnel did not require arms.	In 2009, 5609 cadets and military school children were involved in an operation to bring down drug gangs in Mexico. As the operation did not involve weapons the government insisted that they had not broken international law.
Recruiters are unaware of laws and have recruitment targets.	Although heads of government forces understand the international requirements this is not always passed onto the people who are carrying out the recruitment process. If recruiters are being rewarded for meeting targets, they are more likely to target children.	The Democratic Republic of Congo uses cash incentives to encourage recruiters to increase numbers.
Mistakes about the exact age of individuals can result in children being recruited and used in armed conflict.	A person's age is usually determined by using their birth certificate, but a study carried out by UNICEF discovered that 51 million births are not registered each year and that numbers of unregistered births are higher in areas where conflict is common. Armies will use alternative methods to decide on age, which are often unreliable.	School registration, height and weight have been used to determine age in Uganda, but errors are common.

DON'T FORGET

The International Labour Organisation is a UN specialised agency.

DON'T FORGET

Voluntary recruitment from the age of 16 is permitted within government armed forces but not in non-government groups. This is why you can join the British Armed Forces at 16.

DON'T FORGET

A well-developed answer will include a detailed explanation of your point and an example.

THINGS TO DO AND THINK ABOUT

1 Give three reasons why we should learn about child soldiers.

2 Create a timeline showing the international agreements with regards to child soldiers.

ONLINE TEST

Check how much you have learned about child soldiers online at www.brightredbooks.net/N5ModernStudies.

LIFE AS A CHILD SOLDIER

In this section we are going to investigate why children become soldiers and look at some real-life experiences of child soldiers. Children end up involved in armed conflicts for a range of reasons. To help understand the world issues of child soldiers this section will answer the following key questions:

- Why become a child soldier?
- Why do groups want child soldiers?
- What is it like being a child soldier?

ONLINE

Find out more by following the link to the Child Soldiers International webpage at www.brightredbooks.net/N5ModernStudies.

WHY BECOME A CHILD SOLDIER?

Forced

Rebel groups or recruitment teams from government forces may take children by forcing them or using violence. They might be abducted during the night and dragged away from their families or even taken when they are in school. Families are often threatened with violence or even death if they do not let the children join the group. Zaw Tun from Somalia was forced to join the army as his family could not pay what the recruiters demanded:

'I was recruited by force, against my will [...] army recruitment unit arrived next morning at my village and demanded two new recruits. Those who could not pay 3000 kyats had to join the army ...'

Volunteer

This might be hard to imagine but some children want to join armed groups. Their standard of living may be very low and the promise of food, clothing and shelter can be very appealing when they are struggling to survive from day to day. They might also already be caught up in the conflict and think they would be safer to join a group who may protect them. Their family and friends might already be in the group and therefore they join to stay with them. Some girls join groups to get away from domestic violence at home.

WHY DO GROUPS WANT CHILDREN?

Armed groups recruit children into their ranks because children are very easy to control. They often are too young to understand the conflict and what they are doing, therefore they are easy to manipulate. If children are recruited at a very young age and stay with the group a long time a sense of loyalty is likely to develop. They are much less likely to rebel against leaders and are more likely to follow instructions. Children eat less food and will be happy with a smaller amount of pay therefore they cost the group less money. Children also have a lower sense of danger and are therefore more willing to fight than older soldiers. The risk of children running away is slim because they have nowhere else to go.

WHAT IS IT LIKE BEING A CHILD SOLDIER?

Life as a child soldier is very traumatic. Even though children may have been promised food and shelter, this is often not the case and they continue to live in poverty.

Both boys and girls will receive military training. The development in technology has meant that weapons have became lighter and easier for young children to carry and use, for example the AK47.

contd

Children are taught not only to kill their enemy but also how to capture and torture them. This has long-term psychological effects on children and many struggle to recover from their violent experiences.

Experiences of child soldiers

An account provided by the charity organisation Ajedi-Ka (Projet Enfants Soldats):

'Life forced me to become a child soldier'

A young boy has shared his experiences of being a child soldier with a local charity. He explained that after he was abducted he was trained to kidnap, torture and kill his enemy. This involved learning how to cut off people's ears and feet, and then remove their eyes and finally their hearts. Within the group girls also received army training but were mainly used as cooks or sexually abused. All the children were scared and were not given enough food or medicine when they were sick or injured.

CASE STUDY: DEMOCRATIC REPUBLIC OF CONGO

Since its independence in 1960 the Democratic Republic of Congo (DRC) has been plagued with war and conflict.

The DRC has many natural resources that make it wealthy, such as diamonds, gold, copper, cobalt and zinc. However, the weak infrastructure and corruption of the country has meant that the country has been unable to turn these resources into prosperity. The country has been split into different groups who fight for control over these resources.

In 1994 the Hutu people of Rwanda massacred the Tutsi people and this had a significant effect on the DRC. When the Hutu people lost power in Rwanda they escaped to the DRC and joined forces with the DRC leader Mobutu. Together the National Army and the Hutu groups began to fight against the Tutsi people who lived in the DRC. The Tutsi people were able to seize power from Mobutu and a man named Laurent Kabila became the President. This wasn't the end, however, and the Hutu people, backed by Rwanda's government, continued to fight against Kabila. This war lasted from 1998 to 2003.

It has been estimated that more than 5.5 million people died in the conflict from fighting, starvation or disease.

Despite the DRC signing and ratifying the Optional Protocol in November 2001 both government-backed forces and rebel groups have recruited and used children in these conflicts. Progress was made when the war ended in 2003 and thousands of children were discharged from the armed forces. However, when conflicts broke out again groups turned to children to fill their ranks. An estimated 7000 child soldiers were still members of government forces in 2008.

In 2018, child soldiers continue to be used throughout the Democratic Republic of Congo in in the following provinces:

- North Kivu
- South Kivu
- Ituri
- Tanganyika.

In the Kasi region, UNICEF estimate up to 10,000 children have been recruited for military activity.

Even though the use of child soldiers is illegal the government is not completely enforcing its policies. It has failed to fully explore suspected cases and therefore groups go unpunished.

VIDEO LINK

Watch the short Channel 4 news report 'Diamonds, desperation and child soldiers in the DRC' at www.brightredbooks.net/N5ModernStudies.

FACT

The DRC's name was changed from Congo to Zaire after Joseph Mobutu took over in 1965. It was President Laurent Kabila that named the country the Democratic Republic of Congo.

DON'T FORGET

Child soldiers have many roles other than fighting.

ONLINE TEST

Check how much you have learned about child soldiers online at www.brightredbooks.net/N5ModernStudies.

THINGS TO DO AND THINK ABOUT

1   Write a creative piece about the story of a child soldier. Consider the reasons they became a child soldier, the group they joined and the jobs they had to do.

CHILD SOLDIERS: DEALING WITH THE ISSUE

This section explains the ways groups are trying to solve the problem of children being used in armed conflicts. Many different local and international organisations work hard to stop children becoming soldiers, provide support when they leave armed groups and raise international awareness of the problems.

ONLINE

Find out how Child Soldiers International helps former girl soldiers access education in the DRC at www.brightredbooks.net/N5ModernStudies.

LOCAL RESPONSES

The charity group Ajedi-Ka has been set up within the DRC to concentrate on three areas:

1 poverty   2 environment   3 child soldiers.

In order to tackle the issue of child soldiers the group promotes an awareness of the issue in local communities and provides long-term support to children who have returned from armed groups. Its work therefore deals with the issue of successfully reintegrating children back into their community.

Project: Demobilisation, Reintegration and Rehabilitation of Child Soldiers

This project involves setting up a system of support for children who return home. Within each village that is part of the project a committee for child protection is set up. The aim of the committee is to help children address psychological issues and create positive relationships with those in their community. The charity also funds education projects for child soldiers and helps with the development of small-scale business management so they can become self-sufficient. The project works with the Open Society Institute teaching girls self-confidence and leadership skills. This means they are more likely to be able to break out of the cycle of abuse.

INTERNATIONAL RESPONSES

Child Soldiers International is an international charity working to prevent children from being recruited and used in armed conflict.

It aims to:
- end the military recruitment of children (people below the age of 18) or their use in armed conflict by government armies or non-state armed groups.
- release unlawfully recruited children.
- promote child soldiers' successful reintegration when they return home.
- ensure that child recruiters are brought to justice.

The organisation's work is based on the "child soldiers treaty" – a human rights treaty prohibiting the use of child soldiers, which more than two thirds of the world's governments have pledged to uphold.

Projects

Child Soldiers International has country programmes in Chad, the Democratic Republic of the Congo (DRC), Myanmar and Thailand, where it works in partnership with local activists and organisations to research, analyse and lobby for change – locally, nationally and internationally. It is running a campaign to raise the recruitment age in the UK, one of the few countries which still permits 16 year olds to enter the armed forces. Based on its country work and analysis, Child Soldiers International proposes practical, workable solutions – rooted firmly in human rights law – to support and strengthen the global movement to end the use of children in war.

FACT

The 'Children, Not Soldiers' campaign, which was launched in 2014, aimed to ensure that children across the world were not used in conflict.

THE UN: CHILDREN AND ARMED CONFLICT

Special Representative of the Secretary-General for Children and Armed Conflict: 'To promote and protect the rights of all children affected by armed conflict.'

This UN organisation was set up in 1996 after the World Summit for Children and aims to raise awareness and work with other groups to help children.

So, what does it do?

Sharing information

The UN carries out extensive research and monitoring into crimes involving children in armed conflicts. Its yearly reports focus on the following areas:

- killing of children
- illegal recruitment of children
- sexual abuse involving children
- attacks on schools or hospitals
- kidnapping of children
- humanitarian aid for children.

The findings published in the report will support decisions made by the UN Security Council.

Identifying offenders

The process of identifying offenders has been in place since 2002 and lists groups who are using or illegally recruiting children in armed conflicts. This draws international attention to the groups and forces them to make changes. The 2017 UN Report on Children and Armed Conflict identifies 56 groups and seven state armed forces as recruiting child soldiers in 14 different countries. The only way to get removed from the list is to create an action plan to address the problem.

PROGRESS OF CHILDREN AND ARMED CONFLICT

Compulsory recruitment

Groups have been campaigning to increase the compulsory recruitment age to 18 and many countries have changed their systems to enforce this policy, for example Paraguay, Croatia, Norway and Serbia have all changed their age limits. In addition there are now fewer than 20 countries that recruit individuals aged 16, including India, Iran, Brazil, Canada and the UK.

Success stories

Myanmar, February 2013

Myanmar's government upheld the promise it made to the UN to free child soldiers and help them return home. In February 24 children were released and went back home.

Thomas Lubanga Dyilo, March 2012

Thomas Lubanga Dyilo was heavily involved in the conflict within the DRC and recruited child soldiers as young as 7 to fight for his cause in 2003. In March 2012 the International Criminal Court found him guilty of recruiting child soldiers, torture, rape and ethnic genocide, and was sentenced to 14 years of imprisonment.

THINGS TO DO AND THINK ABOUT

1   You have been tasked with the job of creating a website to highlight the issue of child soldiers. You should include the following points:
    - the number of child soldiers and where in the world they are
    - the laws that exist to protect child soldiers
    - why children join armed forces and what groups use them
    - what life is like for child soldiers
    - what different groups are doing to try and help.

    You should consider the layout of your website, pictures, contact information and any extra features you can think of.

VIDEO LINK

Watch the clip about children and armed conflict for more at www.brightredbooks.net/N5ModernStudies.

ONLINE

Visit the Children and Armed Conflict link for more at www.brightredbooks.net/N5ModernStudies.

DON'T FORGET

You can help raise awareness of child soldiers in your school and contribute to the Child Soldiers International campaign.

ONLINE TEST

Take the 'Dealing with the issue' test at www.brightredbooks.net/N5ModernStudies.

INEQUALITY 1

SUSTAINABLE (GLOBAL) DEVELOPMENT GOALS

The targets outlined in the United Nation's Millennium Development Goals (MDGs) were only partially achieved by the time the initiative reached its 2015 finish date. However, the programme was extremely successful in that it saved tens of millions of lives globally, particularly in sub-Saharan Africa, China and India.

The Sustainable, or Global, Development Goals (SGDs), came into effect in January 2016 and aim to build on the successes of the MDGs. The SDGs also introduce new priorities. The 17 goals are as follows.

1 No Poverty
2 Zero Hunger
3 Good Health and Well-Being
4 Quality Education
5 Gender Equality
6 Clean Water and Sanitation
7 Affordable and Clean Energy
8 Decent Work and Economic Growth
9 Industry Innovation and Infrastructure
10 Reduced Inequalities
11 Sustainable Cities and Communities
12 Responsible Consumption and Production
13 Climate Action
14 Life Below Water
15 Life on Land
16 Peace, Justice and Strong Institutions

In July 2017, UN Secretary-General António Guterres expressed concern about the progress that had been made since the SDGs were launched. He said 'Implementation has begun, but the clock is ticking... the rate of progress in many areas is far slower than needed to meet the targets by 2030'.

We are now going to investigate the issue of extreme hunger and the progress that has been made towards meeting this SDG.

RIGHT TO FOOD

The Universal Declaration of Human Rights Article 25 outlines that everyone has the right to a reasonable standard of living, including enough food.

The problems

There are many different problems associated with food shortages. Although famines have a devastating effect on countries, they only account for 10% of the food shortage related deaths. Many people in the world face everyday challenges accessing enough of the correct food.

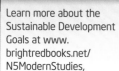

FACT

Although almost 1bn people have been lifted out of extreme poverty since 1999, over 750m people across the globe were still living in an extremely fragile environment in 2013.

ONLINE

Learn more about the Sustainable Development Goals at www.brightredbooks.net/N5ModernStudies,

FACT

A third of all food production, 1.3 billion tonnes, worldwide is wasted each year.

Problem	Definition
Hunger	Consuming fewer than 1800 calories a day
Undernutrition	Shortage of the correct nutrients such as vitamins or proteins. Accounts for 35% of all under-5 mortalities
Malnutrition	Can be either undernutrition or overnutrition. Overnutrition occurs without a correctly balanced diet
Food security	Not having a consistent supply of food
Famine	Declared if: • 20% of the population have access to less than 2100 calories • 30% of children are malnourished • 2/10,000 adult and 4/10,000 child deaths per day

Source: UN Food and Agriculture Organisation, World Food Programme, International Food Policy Research Centre.

contd

The United Nations Food and Agriculture Organisation (FAO) estimated that in 2016, 815 m people across the world were 'chronically undernourished'. Most of these people lived in less developed countries. Lack of sufficient food has a knock-on effect in a person's life: he/she is more likely to get ill, have poor concentration and suffer from fatigue. This means he/she will find it more difficult to, for example, study at school or to get a job.

WHO SUFFERS?

Calculating hunger levels is a complex task involving many different factors. To judge the levels of hunger in the world the International Food Policy Institute created the Global Hunger Index. Countries are rated between 0 and 100, with 0 being no hunger. If a country scores between 20 and 29.9 the situation is 'alarming'; scoring over 30 is classed as 'extremely alarming'.

The index considers the following factors:
- the number of undernourished people in the population
- the number of children under 5 who are underweight
- the mortality rate for children under 5.

Global Hunger Index 2017 Results

- Worldwide levels of hunger and undernutrition have declined between 2000–17.
- 'Deep and persistent inequalities undermine efforts to end hunger and undernutrition worldwide'.
- Almost 20m people are at risk of famine in Nigeria, Somalia, South Sudan, and Yemen.
- South Asia and Africa south of the Sahara have the highest 2017 GHI scores – 30.9 and 29.4 respectively.
- Countries such as Angola, Gabon, and Mali have experienced substantial reductions in undernourishment rates in recent years, achieving rates under 15% as of 2014–16.

REASONS FOR HUNGER

Poor farming

Out of the 815 m hungry people in the world almost 50% of them are farmers who are unable to harvest enough food to either eat or sell.

Conflicts

Countries that are involved in conflicts or experiencing civil wars are much more likely to have high hunger ratings. This is because destroying land and cutting off food supplies are tactics often used by groups.

Gender inequality

Women are more likely to suffer from hunger than men; 60% of chronically hungry people are women. This is a result of poor technology, poor training and being deprived ownership of land, for example in 2009 in sub-Saharan Africa only 40% of women had access to land compared to 85% in Central and Eastern Europe and Central Asia.

FACT

10% of the world's population experience chronic hunger.

THINGS TO DO AND THINK ABOUT

Using the information on these pages, and pages 116–117, create your own hunger campaign. Consider the following points:

- What is your campaign slogan?
- Why should people support your campaign?
- How will you share information about your campaign?
- How could people get involved in your campaign?
- What campaign materials will you produce?

ONLINE TEST

Revise your knowledge of the world issue of hunger at www.brightredbooks.net/N5ModernStudies.

INEQUALITY 2

SDG2: ZERO HUNGER

Although steady progress has been made in tackling global undernourishment, there is still much work to be done. According to the United Nations Development Programme (UNDP) in 2014:

- 795m people were 'chronically undernourished'.
- Over 90m children under 5 were 'dangerously underweight'.
- 25% of Africans still 'went hungry'.

SDG 2 aims to end all forms of hunger and malnutrition by 2030 ensuring all people have access to good nutritious food at all times. The UNDP envisages this will be achieved by:

- Promoting sustainable agricultural practices.
- International co-operation (infrastructure and technology).

ONLINE

Find out more about the inspiring work of the Hunger Project at www.brightredbooks.net/N5ModernStudies

DON'T FORGET

There are many different organisations and charities that are working to overcome global food inequalities.

CASE STUDY: THE HUNGER PROJECT: ERADICATING WORLD HUNGER

The Hunger Project has 380,000 volunteer leaders who work in over 8700 villages in 11 countries in South-East Asia, sub-Saharan Africa and Latin America. Within eight African countries they have set up over 115 epicentre communities. These epicentres are groups of villages that run activities to meet the needs of local people. Each epicentre is given support to get started but then the local people take over and run the activities themselves.

BY THE YEAR 2030 WORLD POPULATOIN IS PROJECTED TO GROW TO AROUND **8.3 BILLION**

Increase investment in agriculture. Build market infrastructure and improve public goods to help raise productivity and rural incomes.

DEMAND FOR FOOD WILL GROW

RISING FOOD DEMAND IS

INCREASING COMPETITION FOR NATURAL RESOURCES

Sustainably manage forests, oceans, water, land and soil – and promote an ecosystem approach to extract greater agricultural yield with fewer inputs.

ABOUT 800 MILLION PEOPLE GO HUNGRY TODAY

Establish social protection systems to improve food access, such as school food and cash transfers. Without nourishment, humans cannot learn, or lead healthy and productive lives.

Develop pro-poor growth strategies in rural areas, focusing on small-scale farmers and the people left furthest behind.

OVERWEIGHT AND OBESITY ARE RISING

MALNUTRITION AFFECTS 1 IN 3 PEOPLE AND ALL NATIONS

Promote nutrition policies, including dietary education, and shift to consumption and production approaches that promote biodiversity and long-term health benefits.

Make food systems more efficient, inclusive and resilient. Improve the way food commodity markets function, and limit extreme food price volatility.

YOUTH NUMBERS ARE RISING FAST IN SUB-SAHARAN AFRICA AND SOUTH ASIA

Diversify rural employment into non-agricultural activities targeting youth to slow their exodus to cities.

Address root causes of inequality. Give poor people access to health, education, land, finance and new technology.

Ensure rural women have equal access to resources, income opportunities, and education.

GENDER EQUALITY IS A PRECONDITION FOR PROSPERITY

ALMOST 4 IN 5 POOR PEOPLE LIVE IN RURAL AREAS

A LARGE SHARE OF FOOD PRODUCED IS LOST OR WASTED

INEQUALITIES ARE INCREASING BOTH WITHIN AND BETWEEN COUNTRIES

Transform agriculture so that it contributes to fossil fuel reduction.

CLIMATE CHANGE IN SUB-SAHARAN AFRICA AND SOUTH ASIA IS JEOPARDIZING CROP AND LIVESTOCK PRODUCTION AND FISH STOCKS

Adopt holistic approaches, such as agro-ecology, agroforestry, climate-smart and conservation agriculture.

CONFLICTS AND CRISES ARE BECOMING INCREASINGLY PROTRACTED

Build the resilience of rural communities to withstand shocks, crises and disasters. Tackle distress migration.

INCREASING GHG EMISSIONS ARE EXACERBATING CLIMATE CHANGE

Build institutions and mechanisms that provide international norms, standards and data, and promote cooperation among countries and partners.

Establish best practices in preventing diseases and anti-microbial resistance that threaten plant and animal production, public health and trade.

2030

ZERO HUNGER

GLOBALIZATION IS INCREASING DEMAND FOR INFORMATION, TECHNOLOGY AND PARTICIPATION

OUTBREAKS OF TRANSBOUNDARY PESTS AND DISEASES ARE GROWING ALARMINGLY

contd

As there are still 815 m hungry people living in less developed countries world hunger is still an issue. Although progress had been made between 2000–15, currently experiencing a decline in famine levels, and some countries are experiencing a rise in their Global Hunger Index rating as a result of conflict. These countries include South Sudan, Nigeria, Somalia and Yemen. According to the World Health Organisation (WHO), 'the prevalence of hunger in countries affected by conflict is 1.4–4.4 percentage points higher than in other countries'.

THE IMPORTANCE OF EDUCATION

Education is something that thousands of children across the world take for granted. They perhaps don't understand its value, as it is part of normal everyday life. However, when you study the impact of education and the levels of access to it across world its importance is very clear.

The significance of education and the inequalities that exist have been recognised by the international community and made a priority in development plans.

Improves health

Children who attend school will also have access to health care. Many schools will administer important vaccinations and provide additional care if a child is unwell. Children will also increase their awareness of health issues, which may prevent them from getting illnesses such as HIV/AIDS.

Decreases poverty

The World Bank has discovered that education is one of the biggest contributing factors to overcoming poverty. They have focused on using education as a pathway out of poverty since 1962. If children receive an education they gain valuable life skills that improve their employment opportunities and allow them to contribute to the economy.

Impact for girls

UNICEF has discovered that girls who have received an education are more likely to produce and raise healthier children. This is because there is a higher chance they will marry at an older age and also decide to have smaller families. Having a smaller family means that the children will be healthier and more likely to receive an education themselves. Educated girls will also have a better knowledge of how to care for their own children and deal with any health problems. Mothers who have been in education have a higher tendency to pursue health information throughout their pregnancy and make sure children are correctly vaccinated.

THINGS TO DO AND THINK ABOUT

What are the different problems caused by the lack of correct food?

 ONLINE TEST

Revise your knowledge of the world issue of education at www.brightredbooks.net/N5ModernStudies.

INEQUALITY 3

INEQUALITIES IN EDUCATION

Access to education

According to UNESCO's 2017–18 Global Education Monitoring Report, 264m children are denied access to education across the world. Out of this total almost 100 m live in sub-Saharan Africa. It has also been discovered that the majority of children that are not in school live in areas affected by conflict or natural disaster.

Equal access

Equal access to education is also a key issue: two out of three countries experience gender inequalities within their education systems, with boys being more likely to attend school than girls, for example in 1990 for every 100 literate males there were 90 females. Although that had improved to 100:95 in 2010, a gender gap still exists. In 2017 two-thirds of the 750 million adults who did not have a basic level of literacy were female. Southern Asia has achieved recent success in tackling adult literacy with the rate rising from 46% in 1990 to 72% in 2016.

Quality of education

Even when children are attending school in less-developed countries there are huge differences in the experiences they have. Schools are often understaffed and overcrowded, for example in the Central African Republic some schools have as many as 84 pupils per class. There is also a shortage of resources: in Cameroon up to 12 pupils may have to share a textbook. Schools are often of a low quality, for example in Chad 75% of schools have no water, sanitation or electricity. If SDG 4 (inclusive and equitable quality education and lifelong learning opportunities for all) is to be achieved, UNESCO believes that:

- 69m new teachers are needed worldwide to reach the 2030 goals.
- $39bn is needed to fill the funding gap.

FIGHTING FOR EDUCATION

UNESCO

The UN specialised agency UNESCO is committed to supporting the development of education across the world. The organisation works with governments and other international groups to try and achieve the fourth SDG.

In 2018, UNESCO is supporting governments by providing policy advice and technical assistance in relation to a number of areas including global citizenship, sustainable development, digital learning, emergencies and crises and female education.

Recent projects include:

- Providing education and psychosocial support to Syrian refugee children.
- Supporting children, youths and adults in South Sudan who have suffered from conflict.
- Giving Guatemalan adolescents a second chance at accessing education.

Case study: Migrant orphans learn with mobile devices in Thailand

'A UNESCO-supported orphanage on the Thai-Myanmar border has given stability to refugee and migrant children along with enhanced learning through mobile devices. The orphanage, The Heavenly Home, started after its founder Lily was asked to take in a six-month old abandoned baby. Today the baby is a happy, healthy 11-year-old

ONLINE

Find out more about UNESCO's work in world education at www. brightredbooks.net/ N5ModernStudies.

VIDEO LINK

Check out UNESCO's YouTube channel for more at www.brightredbooks.net/ N5ModernStudies.

DON'T FORGET

UNESCO stands for United Nations Educational, Scientific and Cultural Organisation.

VIDEO LINK

Watch the clip at www. brightredbooks.net/ N5ModernStudies for more on Education for All.

FACT

Now that more and more children are completing primary school there is an increasing demand for secondary schools.

contd

boy called Sam, one of 73 children who live there fulltime. The orphanage provides children with tablets that contain a UNESCO-designed app featuring over 1,000 learning resources in Thai, Myanmar as well as ethnic languages, and satellite TV with educational programmes and free internet.'

(UNESCO and Education Report 2017)

UNICEF

UNICEF is the biggest organisation that campaigns and supports projects to meet the needs of children across the world. Its aim is to ensure that every child receives the rights outlined in the UN Convention on the Rights of the Child. They have been involved in a range of projects that focus on improving education.

Case study: Work in Uganda

Within the mountains of Karamoja in Uganda there is a collection of villages that are home to the Ik population. Because the area is so isolated, they have limited schools and resources close by. To deal with this problem UNICEF supported the building of a new primary school and projects within the school such as a feeding programme.

LIMITED PROGRESS

Although significant progress was made between 1999 and 2008, when an extra 52m children were enrolled in primary school, there has been little change between 2013–18. As it currently stands, one in every five children are denied access to education. In Afghanistan:

- Two thirds of girls in do not go to school.
- The Taliban have been largely responsible for stopping girls accessing education.
- In 2015, conflict was responsible for almost 370 school closures which affected almost 140,000 students.

Top 10 toughest places for girls' education

Rank	Country
1	South Sudan
2	Central African Republic
3	Niger
4	Afghanistan
5	Chad
6	Mali
7	Guinea
8	Burkina Faso
9	Liberia
10	Ethiopia

(BBC News, 11th December 2017, based on UN figures)

A destroyed school in South Sudan

DON'T FORGET

Education is a universal human right and is outlined in the Universal Declaration of Human Rights, Article 26.

 ONLINE TEST

Revise your knowledge of the world issue of education at www.brightredbooks.net/N5ModernStudies.

 THINGS TO DO AND THINK ABOUT

Consider the following points:

a What do you gain from being in school? Make a list/mind map.

b What would you do if you didn't go to school?

c What would your life be like in 10 years if you had never been to school?

INEQUALITY 4: CHILD MORTALITY

This section addresses the international health inequality of child mortality. Child mortality rates can reveal a range of social and economic problems, including a poor healthcare system. The issue of child mortality has been recognised by the international community and ending preventable deaths of newborns and children under five years of age is SDG #3 which looks to *ensure healthy lives and promote well-being for all at all ages.*

- What is it?
- What areas are affected?
- What progress has been made in overcoming the issue?

WHAT IS IT?

Child mortality is when a child dies before he/she reaches his/her 5th birthday. The rate of child mortality fell by 62% between 1990–2016, dropping from 12.7 million to 5.6 million. UNICEF discovered that 21 children under 5 die every minute from a reason that could be dealt with, for example 70% of child deaths are a result of:

- lack of oxygen when being born
- malaria
- diarrhoea
- illnesses after being born
- pneumonia
- being born too early.

Other reasons also have an impact on rates, including HIV/AIDs, conflict, malnutrition and lack of safe water. These mortality rates can be decreased using simple strategies such as more child vaccinations, more readily available antibiotics, bed nets, food programmes and more support for mothers.

The level of poverty a child is born into affects his/her chances of survival: children born into poverty, rather than wealth, are twice as likely to die before they reach 5 years old. If a mother has received an education, even just to primary level, her children are more likely to live past the age of 5.

VIDEO LINK

Check out the video about child mortality at www.brightredbooks.net/N5ModernStudies.

WHAT AREAS ARE AFFECTED?

There is a significant difference in child mortality rates between developed and less-developed countries. In sub-Saharan Africa for example, one child in 13 dies before his/her fifth birthday, in the developed world, child mortality is one in 189.

As less-developed countries have higher poverty rates and lower access to education it is no surprise that child mortality levels are higher in these regions, for example a child born in Ethiopia is 30 times more likely to die before he/she reaches the age of 5 than a child born in Western Europe.

WHAT PROGRESS HAS BEEN MADE?

According to the findings of a 2017 UN report entitled Levels and Trends in Child Mortality, 'If current trends continue with more than 50 countries falling short of the Sustainable Development Goal (SDG) target on child survival, some 60 million children under age 5 will die between 2017 and 2030 – and half of them will be newborns.'

Deaths per 1000 live births

- > 100
- 75 to 100
- 50 to 75
- 25 to 50
- < 25

contd

The 2015 Millennium Development Goals Report concluded that:

- Between 1990–2015 the global child mortality rate declined from 90 to 43 deaths per 1,000 live births.
- Measles vaccination saved over 15m lives in the thirteen-year period between 2000–13. In 2013, 84% of the world's children received at least one measles vaccination.
- Although there has been a huge reduction in child mortality between 1990–2015, in 2015 16,000 children under-five were still dying each day.

Case study: UNICEF and Angola

As part of the UNICEF Angola Country Programme 2015–19, a Child Survival and Development Programme has been put in place. This plan offers antiretroviral therapy to prevent HIV transmission from mother to child, improves malnutrition training for health workers and ensures that vaccines are available quickly, and stocks do not run out for long periods of time. This is an important programme as Angola has one of the highest child mortality rates of any country in the world and curable diseases such as malaria and diarrhoea are responsible for many deaths each year.

Under-five mortality rate, 1990 and 2015
(deaths per 1,000 live births)

Sub-Saharan Africa: 179 / 86 ↓52%
Oceania: 74 / 51 ↓31%
Southern Asia: 126 / 50 ↓60%
Caucasus and Central Asia: 73 / 33 ↓55%
South-Eastern Africa: 71 / 27 ↓62%
Northern Africa: 73 / 24 ↓67%
Western Asia: 65 / 23 ↓65%
Latin America and the Caribbean: 54 / 17 ↓69%
Eastern Asia: 53 / 11 ↓78%
Developed regions: 15 / 6 ↓61%
Developing regions: 100 / 47 ↓53%
World: 90 / 43 ↓53%

(scale: 0   50   100   150   200)

This image depicts support in Angola in an emergency context.

THINGS TO DO AND THINK ABOUT

1   'Child mortality rates have decreased throughout the world. All regions have decreased child mortality at the same rate and child mortality is no longer an international concern.' UN spokesperson.

Using the information above, explain why the view of the UN spokesperson is selective in the use of facts?

2   In what ways do high child mortality rates have an impact on a country in the long term?

3   You have now studied three of the Sustainable Development Goals. In what ways do hunger and level of education impact on child mortality?

ONLINE

Find out more about the work that UNICEF does in West and Central Africa. at www.brightredbooks.net/N5ModernStudies.

FACT

The consultation surrounding the SDGs was the largest in UN history. 83 countries participated with over 7m people being surveyed.

DON'T FORGET

Sub-Saharan Africa only contains 1.2 bn of the world's population of 7.3 bn therefore the size of its population is not the reason why it has higher child mortality rates.

ONLINE TEST

Revise your knowledge of the world issue of child mortality at www.brightredbooks.net/N5ModernStudies.

SOURCE-BASED QUESTIONS: CONCLUSIONS

It is important that you are able to understand sources and draw your own conclusions about the information. At National 5 level you are expected to be able to draw conclusions based on information from between two and four written or numerical sources. The question will be worth 10 marks.

DON'T FORGET

Remember to only use information from the sources; you should not include any background knowledge.

TOP TIPS

A conclusion is an overall statement about an issue that is supported with evidence. A strong conclusion always has evidence to back it up. Would you believe a point in a debate if there were no evidence to support it?

Your answer should therefore have two parts:
1 your conclusion/overall statement
2 evidence from the sources to support your conclusion/overall statement.

You should try and link information between sources and within sources. A well-developed conclusion will have evidence from more than one source.

You will not achieve full marks unless you provide evidence from the sources to back up your conclusions.

Be careful that you don't just describe the information in the sources. This is a common mistake that candidates make. You will not receive any marks if you just copy the information from the source. To make sure that you don't do this consider the following points:
● What does the information actually show?
● What can you learn from it?

Imagine the points you are asked to make a conclusion about are actually questions. For example:

You should reach a conclusion about each of the following:
● *United Nations membership* = What changes to membership have occurred?
● *Action taken by the United Nations* = What action does the United Nations take?
● *Voluntary agencies and the United Nations* = What relationship is there between voluntary agencies and United Nations?

When practising your conclusion questions try writing the conclusion in one colour and the evidence in another. That way you can easily see if you have included both elements in your answer.

Steps:
1 Read the sources of information that you have been provided with.
2 Read the question: what are you required to make conclusions about?
3 Decide on your overall statement.
4 Decide what evidence you can use to support your point. Make sure you try and link information between sources.
5 Structure your conclusion.

Structure:

A conclusion that can be made about _____ is _____. I think this because

Source 1/2/3/4 states _____. Source 1/2/3/4 also states _____.

EXAMPLE QUESTION

SOURCE 1: Use of the death penalty

Supporters of the death penalty argue that it is an effective deterrent against crime. They state that the tougher the punishment the less likely people are to commit the crime.

The number of countries that have the death penalty as a form of punishment is dropping, but the death penalty is still being used on a global scale. In 2015, 25 countries completed executions; by 2017 this had decreased to 23.

Evidence suggests that China has executed more people than the rest of the world put together. There is no exact figure, as the Chinese government will not share this information. Iran has the second-highest number of executions.

Not all death penalty sentences are carried out within international law, for example Yemen executed two prisoners for crimes they had carried out when they were below the death penalty age limit of 18. Belarus has carried out executions that have gone against the rights of the prisoners under Articles 6, 7 and 14 of the International Covenant on Civil and Political Rights.

In 2015, 1,634 people were sentenced to death in 25 countries. This number dropped in 2017, when 993 people in 23 countries were sentenced to death.

Overall there are almost five times as many countries not carrying out the death penalty as those who do.

SOURCE 2: Executing and non-executing countries

Year	Executing countries	Non-executing countries
2012	21	48
2013	22	59
2014	22	75
2015	25	86
2016	23	96
2017	23	97

SOURCE 3: 2016 executing countries

SOURCE 4: Case study: Belarus and the death penalty

- Belarus is the only country in Europe and Central Asia that continues to use the death penalty as a form of punishment.
- In 2016 evidence indicates that at least four individuals were executed, but information about death penalty cases is kept private therefore the number could be a lot higher.
- Uladzlau Kavalyou and Dzymitry Kanavalau were arrested for suspicion of being involved in bomb attacks in Belarus in 2011. They received unjust trials, which resulted in their execution.
- This case broke international law as neither of the prisoners was given the opportunity to appeal.
- Both prisoners stated that they had been forced to admit to their charges through torture and threats.
- Uladzlau Kavalyou was executed despite the UN Human Rights Committee's orders not to until they had reviewed the case.

Using Sources 1, 2, 3 and 4 above, what conclusions can be drawn about the use of the death penalty as a form of punishment?

You should reach a conclusion about each of the following.

- changes in the use of the death penalty
- the country carrying out the highest number of executions
- Belarus and its use of the death penalty.

Your conclusions must be supported by evidence from the sources. You should link information within and between sources in support of your conclusions.

Your answer must be based on all four sources.

10 marks

(Source: Amnesty International 2011–18)

THINGS TO DO AND THINK ABOUT

Try out the example question above. Remember to use the two-part structure when answering. Your teacher or lecturer will be able to give you advice on your answer.

GLOSSARY

Act

A bill which has received royal assent and become a law

Additional Member System

The voting system used in the Scottish Parliament, which gives voters two votes in the hope of achieving a more proportional overall result

amendments

changes made to bills, usually by parliament

Arab Spring

A series of revolutions against governments of Arab countries

ballot paper

The piece of paper you place your vote on in an election

benefit cap

a limit on the amount of social security payments (benefits) which a person or family can receive from the UK government

benefit fraud

giving false information to the government, to get more social security payments than one is entitled to

benefit trap

when the amount of social security payments one can receive is greater than the amount one would get from working: putting one off trying to get a job

benefits

social security payments from the government

bicameral

A parliamentary system which has two houses, like the House of Commons and the House of Lords in the UK Parliament

Bill

A draft law

BRICS

Brazil, Russia, India, China and South Africa. Up and coming economic world powers.

Cabinet

The most important members of a government; a group of people who assist the Prime / First Minister and are in charge of different government departments

candidates

people who want to be elected

canvassing

going door-to-door to meet voters in an election campaign

capital expenditure

spending money on large projects like bridges and schools

coalition

a government made up of two or more different parties

collective responsibility

the rule that members of a **cabinet** must support the decision in public, even if they disagree with it

Committees

groups of MSPs or MPs (and sometimes members of the House of Lords) who meet to discuss and investigate certain policy areas

constituency

an area which elects an MP or MSP

constituency link

when it is very clear who represents an area in parliament

constituents

people who live in an area represented by an MP or MSP

council tax

a tax which adults must pay to the local council, which pays for local council services like parks and waste collection

crossbenchers

Members of the House of Lords who are not a member of any political party, and are therefore neutral

custodial sentence

being sent to prison or a young offenders' institution as punishment for a crime

debate

when MPs, MSPs or councillors discuss an issue or suggested law; an opportunity for different opinions to be heard

Decision Time

When MSPs vote on all the bills and statements of the day: held in the afternoon

Deforestation
The cutting down or removal of forest trees

democracy
a political system where people are given a say in the decisions made for the country

demonstrations
when people meet to show support for, or opposition to, something or someone

devolution
the passing of power from one part of government to a lower part of government

devolved matters
policy areas the Scottish Parliament gets to make decisions about

disproportional
too large or small in proportion to something else, like when a share of seats lower than the share of votes a party wins in an election

division
a vote in the UK Parliament

election campaigns
the time when political parties and candidates are allowed to try to win votes

electorate
the people allowed to vote in an election

entrepreneurs
people who start up and run businesses

evaluative terminology
words which clearly show the value of something; how big or small it is

favelas
a shanty town in Brazil with poorly built and overcrowded houses

federal republic
a way to run a country where there is one central government which has authority over the whole country and state governments with specific state powers

first-generation immigrants
people who have moved into a country

First Minister's Question Time
the time when MSPs get to ask the First Minister questions about the government's or the First Minister's actions

First Past The Post system
The electoral system used to elect MPs to the UK Parliament

fuel poverty
when after paying for fuel a family has less money than the official poverty line; or when a household needs to spend more than 10% of its income on fuel to maintain a reasonable heat in the home

G20
a group of 19 countries and the EU who come together to improve the world's economy

gang culture
the lifestyle of illegal behaviour which gang members live

general election
When Members of the UK Parliament are elected by the public

glass ceiling effect
the combination of factors which stops many women reaching the top of their professional careers: the top positions can be seen, but something is stopping many reaching it

government
The group of MPs or MSPs who decide how the country will run, after winning the election

House of Commons
the lower house of the UK Parliament, made up of MPs elected by the public

House of Lords
the upper house of the UK Parliament, made up of appointed peers, (elected) hereditary peers, and bishops from the Church of England

human rights
rights that everyone is entitled to

hustings
public meetings where candidates in an election speak in front of, and are asked questions by, the public

hypothesis
an educated guess about what might be found out about a research topic; it can be proven or disproven

ideologies
ideas about how a country should be run

GLOSSARY

industrial action
action taken by members of a trade union designed to disrupt production, like a strike

legislation
laws, at all stage of being passed

lobbying
putting pressure on decision-makers, usually by actually going to meet them in person

local councils
the level of government which makes decisions for their local areas

majority government
when a party wins an election with more than half of the seats in parliament

mandate
the authority to carry out a policy or policies

manifesto
a document containing plans for what a political party will do if they win the election

means-tested
benefit payments which vary depending on your circumstances (usually how much you earn)

media
TV, radio and newspapers as a way of communicating with the public

Millennium Development Goals
a list of 8 goals that were agreed by the members of the United Nations to deal with poverty, hunger, disease, illiteracy, the environment and discrimination against women

minority ethnic
belonging to any ethnic (racial) group which is not white

minority government
when a party wins more seats than any other, but less than half of the seats in parliament, but decides to form a government anyway

minutes
a record of what has been said in a meeting

motion
the topic of a debate

National Minimum Wage
the minimum pay per hour almost all workers are entitled to by law

negative campaigning
when parties or candidates in an election focus on the failings of their opponents, instead of their own strengths

non-custodial sentences
any punishment other than prison received for a crime

occupational pensions
a way of saving for retirement which is arranged by the employer

opposition
all parties other than those in government

parliament
where laws are made

party election broadcasts
TV and radio broadcasts made by political parties to persuade people to vote for them

peers
members of the House of Lords

petitions
a request, usually signed by many people, which is presented to decision-makers

plea
the opportunity the accused has in a trial to say whether they think they are 'guilty' or 'not guilty'

plurality
the single biggest number, but less than half

policy
a course of action proposed by a political party

positive action
the steps an employer can take to encourage people from groups which have previously been discriminated against to apply for jobs

poverty
being extremely poor, which can be defined in many ways

poverty line

a way of measuring poverty: 60% of the median (the middle value if all were lined up) income in the UK

Presiding Officer

the person in charge of the debating chamber in the Scottish Parliament

pressure group

a group of people who share an interest or concern, and want to influence decision-makers in favour of their interest

Prime Minister's Question Time

the time when MPs get to ask the Prime Minister questions about the government's or the Prime Minister's actions

Private Member's Bill

a bill proposed by an MP or MSP who is not a member of the government

proportional

matching in proportion to something else, like when a share of seats matches the share of votes a party wins in an election

prosecute

to carry out legal court action against someone

public sector

the organisations in the country paid for by the government through tax money

Question Time

when MPs or MSPs get to ask government ministers about their actions

quota

the amount of votes required to be elected under the Single Transferable Vote voting system

rebellion

when MPs vote against their party leadership's wishes

recession

when production and trade in a country reduces so a country becomes less wealthy

referendum

a public vote on an issue

remand

to place a defendant on bail or in custody

representative democracy

when people choose people to speak up for them when decisions are made, like MPs or MSPs

reserved matters

policy areas the UK Parliament gets to make decisions about

Royal Assent

when the monarch (King or Queen) officially approves a law; now done automatically

safe seat

a parliamentary seat where the winner is almost guaranteed

sectarianism

behaving in a bigoted or narrow-minded way to a person or people because they follow a different religion

shop steward

a trade union representative in a workplace

Single Transferable Vote

the voting system used for Scottish local council elections, which is designed to give each area 3 or 4 representatives to each area, and give proportional results

Speaker

the person in charge of the debating chamber in the UK Parliament

state pension

the money every elderly person above a certain age receives from the UK government

surgeries

open meetings held by representatives (like MPs, MSPs and councillors) where members of the public can raise concerns

surplus votes

votes which a local council election candidate has left over after already being elected – above the quota

tactical voting

when voters vote for a candidate other than their favourite, just to avoid their least-favourite candidate winning

GLOSSARY

tax avoidance
legally taking action to lower the amount of tax you have to pay

trade unions
organisations which represent groups of workers

turnout
the share of people who could have voted who did vote

unicameral
a parliamentary system which has one house, like the Scottish Parliament

United Nations
an international organisation dedicated to promoting peace, security and human rights

verdict
the final decision in a court case; usually 'guilty' or 'not guilty'

ward
a local council area, which elects 3 or 4 local councillors

wasted votes
votes for candidates who are not elected

welfare state
a system whereby the government takes responsibility of protecting the health and well-being of its citizens